BECOMING KID QUIXOTE

A TRUE STORY OF BELONGING IN AMERICA

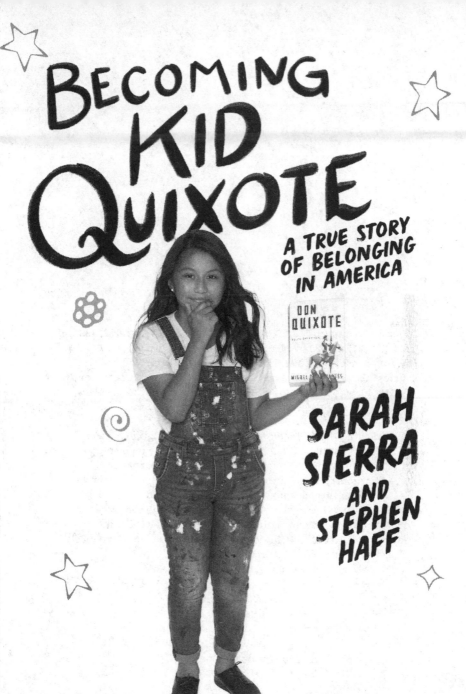

DON QUIXOTE

MIGUEL CERVANTES

SARAH SIERRA

AND STEPHEN HAFF

HARPER

An Imprint of HarperCollinsPublishers

ISBN 978-0-06-294326-2

The artist used Adobe Photoshop to create
the illustrations for this book.
Typography by Carla Weise
20 21 22 23 24   PC/LSCH   10 9 8 7 6 5 4 3 2 1
❖
First Edition

To Quixotes everywhere . . .

Contents

1

About Me

Hi! I'm Sarah. I am ten years old, and I live in Brooklyn, New York, with my parents, my brother, my three little sisters, and *lots* of cousins and aunts and uncles. Have you ever been to Brooklyn? It's a part of New York City. Everyone thinks that means it's full of skyscrapers, but where I live it's more like a neighborhood. Most of the buildings only have a couple of apartments in them—not skyscrapers at all. But even though Brooklyn is not near Times Square or the Empire

State Building, my part of New York City can still be pretty exciting.

How many kids have performed at *City Hall*? That's right; last year my friends and I were in a show there. We've also done our show at a consulate, at colleges and universities, and at some big office buildings—so I *have* been up in a skyscraper.

You might have guessed by now that I really like acting. A lot of people are surprised by that, because when I'm not performing, I can be pretty quiet. In school I would rather do my work silently than talk all the time. Everyone thinks that actors have to be loud and dramatic, but some actors aren't that way in real life. Like me. There are a lot of differences between the character I play and the person I am. When I'm acting, I play Don Quixote, a man who imagines he is a heroic knight. Don Quixote is bold, adventurous, and *hates* dresses. That's who I am onstage. In real life, I am more thoughtful, and I like dresses okay. Especially if they are turquoise—that's my favorite color.

Our show is called *The Traveling Serialized Adventures of Kid Quixote* because we travel to

different places to perform. "Serialized" means that we perform one part of the story at a time—like an episode in a TV series. We practice in our neighborhood three days a week at a place called Still Waters in a Storm, unless we are traveling for a show. It's called Still Waters in a Storm because it's a place that is safe. If you were in a boat in a storm, you would look for still waters, for water that is calm and peaceful so that your boat doesn't tip. That's why Stephen, our director, called this place Still Waters in a Storm—so that kids know that when they are there, they don't have to worry. At Still Waters in a Storm, we never let each other's boats sink. When we go out and perform, we call our acting group Still Waters, too.

My apartment is just around the corner from Still Waters, so my sister Cleo and I walk there together. My other two sisters are too little to come with us, and my older brother doesn't like performing as much as I do, so it's just Cleo and me.

Still Waters is on the first floor of a building with five floors. The whole place is one big room, with a couch, tables and chairs, and a *lot* of bookcases. I once heard Stephen say that there are thousands of books at Still Waters—adventure, fantasy, books about sisters, books about pirates and cathedrals, and lots of comics and graphic novels. There's a keyboard in the back and a big window in the front that we decorated with colored tissue paper—when the sun shines through the paper, the windows look like stained glass and cast rainbow patterns all over the room.

When we get to Still Waters, Cleo and I each play with our friends for a little while, until all the kids have arrived. Sometimes while she waits, Cleo reads Raina Telgemeier books, like *Sisters* or *Smile*. Those are her favorite books. I mostly play with my cousins Bernadette and Paulo and my friend Wendy. Sometimes we read *Calvin and Hobbes* comics together, sometimes we draw, and a lot of times we just talk. Usually my friends Rex, Santiago, Joseph, and Percy are playing soccer. If it's nice out, they get to go to the sidewalk out front, but if it's raining or cold, they play inside—and then watch out for flying balls!

The teenagers are usually the last ones to arrive. Joshua, Alex, and Ruth are in high school, and all three of them are really good at singing and acting. Alex knows how to play the ukulele and the guitar. Ruth plays the ukulele, too.

Having the teenagers there is one of my favorite parts of Still Waters. It's like a family—there are little kids, middle kids like me, teenagers, and grown-ups. Like a big family that all fits in one room with thousands of books and colored-paper glass.

Today we are writing a new section of our show, because we don't only act and sing—we actually write our own play, section by section. When we have performances, we act all the parts we've written so far, but because the show is serialized, we are always adding new installments to the series. Once we have written and rehearsed a new part, we add it to our next performance.

Our show is inspired by *Don Quixote*, a book about a regular man in Spain who convinces himself that he is a knight, written by an author named Miguel de Cervantes over four hundred years ago. I play Don Quixote, this man who really, *really* wants to help people, only he is so clumsy that sometimes he ends up causing more problems than he solves. In the book, Don Quixote rides around the countryside in Spain (which is in Europe, on the other side of the Atlantic Ocean from New York). He travels with his horse, Rocinante, and his best friend, Sancho Panza, looking for people to rescue. Wendy plays Sancho Panza, and Rocinante the horse is played by a stuffed animal. *Don Quixote* is one of the oldest and most important books ever published, and even though it was written so many hundreds of years ago, there's a lot that Miguel de Cervantes understood: like how hard it is to help people and make the world a better place, even if you want to with all your heart.

When we write our play, we use the events of Don Quixote, but sometimes we change the story so that it makes more sense to kids living right now. For example, in the book, Don Quixote does everything he does because he loves a woman named Dulcinea. He wants to be a better knight and fight harder for justice so he can live up to Dulcinea's expectations. When we started writing our version of Don Quixote, we talked about how most of us are too young for dating or serious relationships, and it didn't really make sense to

us why Don Quixote would do so much for Dulcinea. But all of us *do* really love our parents. We
want to do well in school to make our parents
proud. Our favorite part of performing is when
our parents clap for us. We wish this world were
better and easier so that our parents didn't have
to spend so much time working, especially when
they are tired. So we changed Dulcinea to Mami,
and at the beginning of every show, I say to the
audience: "Mami, everything I do is because I love
you so much in my heart."

We also don't always use the same names as
the characters in the book. Stephen wants us to
really *be* the characters, so even though I do a lot
of the same things Don Quixote does in the book,
in the play they just call me Sarah. It's a lot easier
to feel like I'm Sarah, fighting bad guys to help my
mami, than it is to pretend that I'm an old knight
from four hundred years ago trying to impress his
Dulcinea! We don't have fancy costumes or sets
either—that way, we can perform in lots of different locations without needing an auditorium, and
it's not as intimidating. When we are performing

as ourselves, with our own names, it's not really acting. It's more like playing pretend with your family.

Once all the kids arrive, Stephen calls everyone over to the tables, which we line up to make one big table in the center of the room. Everyone

sits around the table. There are no lines or rows. It doesn't matter if you are a teenager or if you are the littlest kid, everyone sits in the group together. Today we are writing a scene where Don Quixote rescues people who were thrown in prison unfairly. Before we start adapting this scene for our show, Stephen passes out folded pieces of light brown construction paper to everyone at the table.

The letters.

A few weeks ago, we all wrote letters to girls at an Immigration and Customs Enforcement (ICE) detention center. ICE detention centers are basically like prisons, except the people inside haven't committed any crimes. The people are

trapped there because they are "undocumented immigrants" and they don't have "papers." Not having "papers" means you can't vote. If you get sick it can be hard to see a doctor. Your boss can get away with not paying you enough money, even if you work hard. It's not always fair how some people can get papers and other people can't. I've always had papers—a little *baby* in the United States gets papers just by being born. Sometimes immigrants (people from other countries who live in the United States) can get papers because a family member helps them, or they get permission because the country they came from isn't considered safe anymore. But that doesn't always happen. Some people—no matter how great they are and how hard they work—never get papers, and they stay undocumented. Undocumented people work hard for the United States—they grow crops, build buildings, raise kids—but it's like no one cares. They can still be treated poorly. Worst of all, someone who is undocumented can get captured by ICE—the Immigration and Customs Enforcement people. ICE might send them

back to the country they came from, even if it's dangerous, even if they don't even *know* anyone in that country, even if they have a job to do here in the United States. Or they could be stuck. Like the girls we wrote letters to.

These girls are mostly from Guatemala, which is in Central America, south of Mexico. They are teenagers. But they are stuck in a detention center, waiting to hear what will happen to them, instead of going to school. It can be very boring and sad at the detention center, so Stephen encouraged us to tell them stories that would help cheer them up. I drew a unicorn on my letter. Santiago wrote about a time he went to see a soccer game (of course—Santiago never misses a chance to talk about soccer). Today, we got to read the letters they wrote back to us.

I unfold my letter. It's from a girl named Dolores. She has beautiful, neat handwriting. It's in Spanish, which luckily I speak because I am bilingual. Her note is short and doesn't tell me much about what she has been doing, but it sounds like she really liked getting a letter. She tells me, *Que*

Dios te bendiga—"May God bless you." Stephen tells us to keep our letters safe, because they are priceless treasures. I put mine in my pocket. I hope Dolores gets out of detention soon, and I hope she gets to stay here. I think she would be a good person to have as a neighbor.

Now it's time to work on the prison scene for our show. I look around the table. I look at my friend Wendy and my cousin Bernadette. I look at my sister Cleo with the other little kids. I look at the soccer boys. I look at Stephen, our director. We all know *exactly* how we will adapt the prison scene. The prison will be like a detention center, and we will share the girls' stories in our play so that everyone who watches us perform will know their tale. Then I, Kid Quixote Sarah, will free the prisoners!

❁ ❁ ❁

2

Día de los Muertos

It is late October, and it is gray out when Cleo and I walk home from Still Waters. The telephone and electrical wires look like black spiderwebs crisscrossing the sky, and everyone around us walks quickly because it is getting cold out. We pass row houses and apartments, a taquería and a coffee shop, then turn onto our block. Our building is right on the corner. Inside, we go up a long flight of stairs. At the top of the stairs, my mom is holding open the door to our apartment. She's carrying my baby sister, Alma, while my other little sister

Natalia and my brother, Diego, are doing home-work in the back of the apartment. It smells like someone has been making flautas. If you have never eaten flautas, you should try them. They are chicken rolled up in tortillas, and they are *yummy*.

Soon it will be Halloween, and right after that it will be Día de los Muertos, which is an impor-tant holiday where I live in Brooklyn. There's a party in my favorite park, and different people who work in my neighborhood have booths where they give out information—even the dentist sets up a stand for Día de los Muertos! Día de los Muertos is all about celebrating your ancestors who have died, but it's not really sad. It's more of a happy celebration, like in the movie *Coco*, which Cleo and I love to watch.

After we eat, my dad helps us prepare for Día de los Muertos. My grandfather died when my dad was only a little kid, so my dad likes to remember him at Día de los Muertos even though my sib-lings and I never got to meet him. My dad takes out a picture of him, and we put out things like bread, water, fruit, and tequila near the photo.

Some days, my dad burns incense that is earthy and flowery and makes our apartment smell good. My mom says that the water is an offering for anyone who is struggling or having a hard time. Putting out the water is like a special prayer that those struggling will be okay and have enough to eat and drink.

I think that Stephen would say that my dad is very devoted. At Still Waters, we talk a lot about *devoción*. When you are devoted to something or someone, you give yourself to them completely— you spend your time on them and you focus your attention on them. All of us actors are devoted to our performance of *Kid Quixote* because we spend so much time working on writing and rehearsing our show. My parents are devoted to family. I know my dad has a lot of *devoción* because he never forgets his father, no matter how much time passes. Some years, he even travels to Mexico to visit his father's grave. My mom has a lot of *devoción* to all of us: she comes to our performances and makes us eat healthy and checks that we do our homework on time.

For the Día de los Muertos celebration in the park, a lot of people dress up as Catrinas or Catrines, which are skeletons but not spooky ones. Catrinas and Catrines have white face paint with black around the eyes, like a skeleton, but they also have colorful designs on their faces. They can wear suits and dresses and put hats and flowers in their hair. I love dressing up as Catrina because my dad is amazing at painting faces. When he helps me dress up, I am the most elaborate Catrina in the neighborhood, and even though our faces are painted, everyone knows it's my siblings and me because no one else has face paint as detailed as us.

I want to be an extra-good Catrina this year because I have a reputation to defend. Earlier in October, we celebrated Hispanic Heritage Month at my school, and everyone got to dress up as an important person from Hispanic history. My family is from Mexico, so my first idea was to be Frida Kahlo, the famous Mexican painter. Frida liked to paint self-portraits, sometimes with a monkey on her shoulder, sometimes with a tiara of flowers on her head. Even though hard things happened to her, including having her leg crushed in an accident, Frida kept painting. She makes people proud to be Mexican, so I thought she would be a good choice for school. But a lot of the kids from my school are *also* Mexican, and they *also*

planned to dress up as Frida. I thought maybe I should be someone unique, so I kept brainstorming other people, but really, Frida was my favorite. I loved the tiara of flowers she wore, and I still wanted to dress up

as her even if other people were too

Luckily, I had my family to help make sure that even if I was one of many Fridas, I could still stand out. First my dad promised he would do my makeup to look exactly like Frida. Then my mom and I went to the dollar store and bought a big bag of artificial flowers, the kind people use to make wreaths and decorate. One by one, we glued the flowers into the shape of a tiara, just like the one Frida had. Then my parents showed me lots of pictures of Frida—not just the famous ones you see everywhere, and not just the ones with the crown of flowers, but a painting where she has a *resplandor*, which is a special kind of Mexican headdress. When Frida painted herself wearing a *resplandor*, it didn't just have flowers—a special veil hung from the flowers to her shoulders, framing her face. My mom cut fabric and attached it to the flowers we glued so that I had a *resplandor*, which I was sure no one else at school would have. The last detail was my clothing—I had a blouse I could wear, but no skirts that were anything like what Frida wore. Frida's skirts were long and full and flowing, with bright colors and patterns. I looked online and found a skirt that was *perfect*— it was like the skirt had been taken straight from one of Frida's paintings—but it was so expensive there was no way we could get it. I could tell my dad was tempted because we had already worked so hard on my Frida costume, but my mom and I are resourceful. We walked all over the neighborhood until we found a thrift store with a skirt that wasn't *exactly* like the one we had seen on the internet, but it was pretty close.

The day I went to school wearing my Frida costume, I felt like I had both my parents with me because they had worked to make my beautiful costume. My friends and my teachers were so impressed. We all lined up in the gymnasium and got a turn to come up to the front and show off our costumes. I got more applause than anyone.

So on the day of the Día de los Muertos celebration, I hold extra still while my dad paints my Catrina face. I make sure my little sisters do too. I want us all to look like the real thing so that everyone will know that our family always has the best costumes and makeup. Finally, we're ready to go to the park.

When we get there, kids are running around and adults are saying hello to one another and visiting the different stands. Some of the stands are for ancestors, and they are decorated with flowers and candles and piles of fruit and corn. I run to find my friends—it's hard to tell who is who because there are so many Catrinas and Catrines! I find my friend Talia, who plays a bully in *Kid Quixote* (she is nice in real life though), and we run to get Jarritos from one of the stands. Jarritos is a type of Mexican soda that comes in many different flavors—my favorites are lime, pineapple, or mandarin.

A mariachi band begins to play. The mariachis are dressed up in black clothing with gold embroidery and hats with big, wide brims. There are violinists, different types of guitars, and trumpets, and people stop to listen to them, or to dance in front of them. While the adults dance and clap, Talia and I wander over to a stand where they sell alebrijes, little paper-mâché statues of mythological animals.

"If you were an alebrije, what would you be?" Talia asks me.

I look at the different alebrijes. Some of them look like jaguars with flying wings. Others look like roosters with claws. Almost any animal you can imagine could be an alebrije. Once, my abuela Beatriz was coming to visit from Mexico and she packed her suitcase with alebrijes to bring to my siblings and me, but they got taken away at the airport. I've always wondered what kind of alebrije I would have gotten, and which ones Cleo and Diego would have gotten. My abuela was going to let us decide which one was for which person. Would I have gotten a brave jaguar or a gentle cat? Would I have gotten one with wings? But since they all got taken away at the airport, I'll never know which one could have been mine.

"I think I would be a horse mixed with a dolphin," I tell Talia finally. "The kind of horse that could fly." When I was really little I used to think all horses could fly, but of course now I know they can't. But still, I like to think of being a strong horse, flying over everything and crossing distance quickly. I would make it easier for my abuela Beatriz to come from Mexico, and for me to go see her there. I once read that dolphins communicate underwater and that each dolphin has its own special sound so that the other dolphins can find it. If I were a dolphin mixed with a flying horse, I could fly back and forth from Mexico to Brooklyn, and my family and I would always be able to find one another.

3

Rehearsals

By the end of November, we have finished writing the prisoner scene of *The Traveling Serialized Adventures of Kid Quixote*, and then we have to practice, practice, practice. In February, when school has winter break, we are going on tour, like a real acting troupe or a band of musicians. We are going to be visiting two different universities in New York City, and two outside of New York City. In New York City, we will take the subway from Brooklyn to Manhattan. The subway will cross a river, and we'll see the tall buildings in Manhattan from the windows. In Manhattan, we will perform for the students at Hunter College and Columbia University. Outside of New York City, we are going to take our own coach bus to visit Philadelphia, Pennsylvania, and perform at Drexel University, and then to New Haven, Connecticut, to Yale University. We'll see a lot of different places in one week, and I think it's pretty cool that college students will watch our performances.

One Saturday morning when Cleo and I get to Still Waters, Kim and Tina are setting up a music stand by the keyboard. Kim is our music director at Still Waters. Just like Stephen directs the writing and acting, Kim directs the singing for the show. Her friend Tina sometimes comes to help us as well. Kim and Tina are both professional musicians and composers, and they helped us write the music for our scenes.

To write the music for *The Traveling Serialized Adventures of Kid Quixote*, Kim told us to think about our emotions at different parts of the show. When Don Quixote and his sidekick leave for an adventure, we told Kim that it was a happy, exciting part. When Don Quixote finds the kids at the detention center, we told Kim that it was a very sad part. Kim would play a few different bars of music for each emotion and ask us if it sounded right. Little by little, we composed the songs for our show. In the spring, Kim is going to help us record an album of all of us singing the music together.

When everyone arrives at Still Waters, we gather around Kim and Tina's keyboard to warm up our voices. When we do these exercises before we sing, it makes our vocal cords more flexible.

We can sing louder and longer without sounding scratchy. We sing a scale that goes,

The lips, the teeth, the tip of the tongue
The lips, the teeth, the tip of the tongue
The lips, the teeth, the tip of the tongue.

We sing the same scale faster and faster until we are singing it at light speed, each time trying to make sure we actually move our lips, show our teeth, and tap the tip of our tongue against the back of our teeth. We do that a lot of times. Once Kim decides we are warmed up enough, it's time to rehearse.

Because we are always performing in different places (these are *traveling* adventures, after all), we keep our set simple. We push the tables out of the way, then arrange the chairs in rows. We can always count on the spot where we are performing to have at least chairs, and the space in front of the chairs is our stage. Everyone gathers the props they will need: the little kids get flowers and sheep hats, Ruth gets her ukulele, and I get a big, heavy copy of the actual *Don Quixote* book. Paulo, my cousin who is one grade ahead of me in school, grabs two puppets off the shelf. We are almost ready.

The other kids sit on the floor, at the foot of the chairs where the audience will be sitting when it's an actual show. Stephen tells them to sit up straight and focus their attention on the center of the stage. If they do that, then the audience will follow their gaze.

I am sitting in the center of the stage. When Stephen says, "And action," I begin to turn the pages of my big copy of *Don Quixote*. Everything is so quiet that for a minute I don't want to breathe— it sounds so loud without everyone talking around me. I turn the pages of the book three times, and then the singing begins.

* * *

De claro en claro
de turbio en turbio
leyendo, imaginando, y creyendo

From starlight to starlight
from shadow to shadow
reading, imagining, and believing

Those are the words that describe what Don Quixote does in the book: he stays up too late reading stories about knights traveling the countryside, and he starts imagining that he could be a real knight. The longer he imagines it, the more he starts to believe it. Eventually he believes what he imagines so strongly that he decides to leave home for an epic adventure. In our play, we pretend that instead of an old man reading too many stories about knights, Kid Quixote stays up late reading with a flashlight under the covers. Kid Quixote reads so much that she also starts to believe she could be a knight and rescue people. Finally, she sneaks away from the school bus stop for *her* epic adventure.

Tabitha, who plays my mom in the play, comes on the stage after the first song. She tells me to put my book away and go to sleep. In the next scene, it is morning and Tabitha helps me get ready for school. She helps me pack a backpack, and I put the school skirt on over my jeans and pretend it's a flowery dress. While we get ready, we sing "Pin-pon es un Muñeco," a nursery rhyme that moms sing to little babies. Then it's time for my first solo part of the show. As soon as Tabitha walks away, I say to the audience, "I hate dresses!" and stuff the skirt into my backpack. (This is why it is called acting: I don't really hate dresses that much.)

I tell the audience I want to have adventures and rescue people in need. I call to my brave stallion, Rocinante, and Joseph throws Rocinante my way—a stuffed animal! We count on the audience to imagine it's a real horse. Besides, even if they aren't quite sure if this Kid Quixote character is for real, that's sort of the point—because Don Quixote wasn't *really* a heroic knight, he just pretended to be. And maybe by pretending, he becomes just a little bit heroic in real life.

Rocinante and I find our first person to rescue—a farmworker who has not been paid and is being beaten by his boss. At first, this is a really upsetting part of the show because Talia, who also plays the farmworker, is shouting "Ouch!" But after I step in and stand up to the boss, played by Stephen, it gets less frightening, and even a little funny. You see, Stephen doesn't speak much Spanish. He knows enough to get by, but he mixes words up all the time. When we were working on the script for our show, we all teased him. *Don Quixote* was written in Spanish, so without all of us kids helping Stephen, it would have been harder to adapt it into a show! We worked some of Stephen's mistakes into the script to lighten the mood. For example, in *Don Quixote* the cruel master

claims to be punishing the worker because the worker lost a sheep. The word for "sheep" in Spanish is "*oveja*" but Stephen kept mixing it up with "*abeja*," which sounds similar but means something totally different—a bee! Now it's part of the play, and Talia holds up stuffed animal sheep and bees every time Stephen mixes them up in the show.

Talia is still sad even after getting rescued, so Paulo cheers her up with his puppets. Do you want to hear one of the jokes Paulo makes? He asks:

"What do sheep say on Christmas?"

"Fleece Navidad!"

Get it? Instead of *Feliz* Navidad (Merry Christmas), the sheep say *Fleece* Navidad! After that scene, all the other kids put on their sheep hats and sing, "Fleece Navidad, baa baa baa baa baa!"

After a few adventures, Don Quixote in the book decides he needs a sidekick, so he asks Sancho Panza to join him on his adventures. In the play, I ask my friend Wendy. At first she says she has too much homework, but finally I convince her. Except she insists on making a packing list first! Here are the things she decides to bring on our fictional adventure:

We need blankets, cookies, baby carrots,
   washed and peeled
Fill up our backpacks—mi panza must be
   satisfied!

That last line is sort of a joke, because Miguel de Cervantes meant the name Sancho Panza to be funny. "Sancho" is a regular name, but "Panza" means "stomach" in Spanish, and in *Don Quixote*, Sancho Panza is always worrying about practical things like food while Don Quixote is talking about knights and giants and wizards. Wendy does a great job acting the part of Sancho Panza, thinking of all the practical things you need and making the audience laugh at how detailed her list is, while I, Kid Quixote, am ready to just head out unprepared. Then she adds even *more* to her packing list:

Arroz con habichuelas y pernil
flashlights, chocolate, Quaker Oatmeal
keys in case I need to go back home
and if I'm homesick, I have a bunch of
    toronjil.

Pretty good list, right? You can always count on Wendy! Of course, we all wrote those lines together and came up with a list of everything we would bring ourselves if we went on an adventure. *Arroz con habichuelas y pernil* are essential—rice with beans and ham—and I think chocolate would be pretty important on an adventure too. The line about toronjil always makes everyone laugh. Toronjil is a type of herb with a lemony scent. You use it to make tea, and lots of people's moms give it to them when they are sad or sick. Not quite as exciting as chocolate, but if you need something to make you think of your mom when you are home-sick, toronjil will definitely work. My mom makes it for us with ginger, which makes it lemony and spicy at the same time.

Finally, we get to the new part of the play, where Don Quixote rescues the prisoners. This is the scene we wanted to adapt to include the stories of the undocumented girls in the detention center. The kids who will play the prisoners line up in a row. One by one, I sing to them:

¿Cuál es tu nombre? *What is your name?*

Cleo plays the littlest prisoner. When I first sing to her, she doesn't respond at all. She just looks at me with big round eyes. That's part of the play, so the audience knows that she is small and scared. Then I ask, very gently:

What did you do?
Why are you here?

Another one of the prisoners, played by Paolo, responds, "She didn't do anything wrong. She's here because she's an immigrant."
So this time I ask the little prisoner:

Where is your home?

Now, finally, Cleo opens her mouth and sings her song, which we wrote from what we all knew about Mexico:

A rainbow house with a silver roof where
the sun will always shine.

Cleo sings beautifully. The problem is you can barely hear her. She can be so quiet sometimes.

I get how Cleo is feeling. I didn't used to say very much, and at school I think it's still a good idea to just focus and not turn around and talk to your friends instead. But acting is different from being in school—you have to be loud enough so that the audience can hear you.

I worry that Cleo is too young. I have been coming to Still Waters for years, but Cleo only just started. Maybe she shouldn't have a solo in this show. I pick some fuzz out of Cleo's hair. She's my little sister. I want her to have the part, but I also want everyone in the audience to be able to hear her beautiful song. If people can't hear Cleo sing, then they'll never hear the heartbreaking story of the undocumented girls. If people don't hear the girls' stories, then they won't know that we have to *do* something about how unfairly people who don't have papers are treated.

"Cleo, you have to be louder," I hiss at her.

Cleo looks at me wide-eyed, but she doesn't say anything. This time she's not acting—she's nervous!

Stephen asks if Cleo wants help singing her

solo from the other kids, but Cleo shakes her
head. She wants to do it. With a big sigh, I promise everyone that I will help Cleo practice. By the
time our sister rehearsals are done, I hope you'll
be able to hear Cleo in outer space.

4

Our Lady of Guadalupe

In between school, rehearsals at Still Waters, and helping Cleo get louder, it's December before I know it. Our neighborhood is decorated with Christmas wreaths, and the store displays are filled with Santa Clauses, presents under the tree, and tinsel. Of course I love Christmas, but there's another very important day in December: the Feast of Guadalupe. On December 12, people all over America—North America and South America— celebrate Guadalupe, the patron saint of all

43

America. Guadalupe is especially important to Mexicans, because that's where humans encountered her.

Most people know that María (some people call her Mary) was the mother of Jesus. But not everyone knows that when María died two thousand years ago, she didn't just disappear into the back of a church somewhere. Catholics today believe that María appears to human beings in special moments throughout history. Five hundred years ago, María appeared in Mexico in the shape of Guadalupe.

She didn't appear to a king, or to a wealthy man, or to a European-looking person. Instead, María chose to appear to an Aztec man named Juan Diego. She spoke to him not in English, and not in Spanish, but in Nahuatl, a language spoken by a lot of Aztec people in Mexico (Aztec people are the ones who lived there before the Europeans conquered Mexico). My mom knows some Nahuatl, and maybe someday I'll learn a little bit too.

Juan Diego lived at a time when Europeans were terrorizing Aztec people, killing them, enslaving them, and forcing them to speak

Spanish instead of Nahuatl. When María spoke to Juan Diego in his own language, she sent the world a message that his words and his story were worthy and important and that God loved him just as much as any colonizer.

If December 11 is on a Friday or Saturday, we go to a special mass and pray to Guadalupe at 11:00 p.m. My mom doesn't let us go if it's on a school night, but otherwise we leave our house late at night, when the streets have been dark for hours, and gather in the church with many other families. When I'm in the church at night, I feel a little bit sad—that Jesus died, that Mary was sad, and that everything is cold and dark outside—but also happy at the same time, because it's a celebration. At exactly midnight, we all sing a song called "Las Mañanitas" to Guadalupe. Here is how the song goes:

> Despierta, niña despierta
> mira que ya amaneció
> ya los pajaritos cantan
> la luna ya se escondió

Wake up, my dear, wake up now
see the sun rising up
the little birds are singing
the moon has already set.

It's a song that you sing for the people you love the most: parents sing it to kids on their birthdays, and people in love sing it to one another to show their feelings. We all sing it to Guadalupe on her feast day, and when I hear everyone in the church singing it together I think about how Guadalupe is *everyone's* mother—rich people and poor people, no matter who you are she loves you—and I feel a big swooping feeling inside.

The next day is December 12, and we wake up a little sleepy but ready to celebrate Guadalupe's official feast day. The day is extra special in my family because Cleo was also born on December 12!

My dad gets down a small statue of Guadalupe and puts her on top of the kitchen table. She comes in a big wooden box with windows and a little doorknob in the front, so you can look at Guadalupe without accidentally messing up her

veil, which is green and decorated all over with flowers. At the bottom of the box, near Guadalupe's feet, are beautiful angels.

We celebrate both Guadalupe and Cleo at the same time, so there is usually cake in our apartment on December 12. My cousins—especially Lucas and Aldo and Bruno, who like to be silly— always dare Cleo to shove her face in the cake (they claim it's good luck), but so far Cleo has always gotten through her birthday cake-face-free. Which is lucky, because no one would want to eat the cake if she actually did put her face in it!

During the day on December 12, we also go to a different church, where we watch dances representing all the different regions of Mexico. Just like the United States is divided into states, in Mexico there are different states too: Puebla, Oaxaca, Chiapas, and Durango are some of the most famous. My parents are both from Puebla, which is in the southern part of Mexico. Each region has different traditional dances that get performed at celebrations, with different costumes and music. There's the Dance of the Chinelos and

the Concheros dance, and each one has a special costume and specific moves.

The dancers representing Puebla do a dance called *La Danza de los Tecuanes*, or the Jaguar Dance. Want to know a secret? When I was little I was afraid of the Dance of the Tecuanes. There's one dancer who dresses up as a jaguar. He wears pants and a shirt with yellow splotches like a real jaguar, and a big papier-mâché mask. His mask shows all the jaguar's teeth, and his big red tongue. He carries a whip that he cracks at the other dancers. He moves his feet and his head as if he were a real jaguar, ready to pounce. The other dancers wear wide-brimmed hats and masks depicting human faces with long beards. One person leads the dance by playing a high-pitched flute. The dancers form two lines, and the jaguar cracks his whip. The dancers circle the jaguar, who now acts like he is angry and ready to gobble up the dancers. Then the dance ends, and you remember that the jaguar isn't real and won't actually attack anyone. But while the music is going and the dancers are moving their feet, you are not so sure.

The first time I saw the Dance of the Tecu-anes, I was so scared. My mom says my mouth was hanging open and I cried so loudly she thought we would get kicked out! It was a *tremendo llor-adero*, which means a very big crying fit. Someone had thought it would be a good idea to put all the kids up front so we could see better, but little-kid me did *not* think that was a good idea and tried to hide. I asked my mom why people had let monsters in and my mom just said, "*¡Espera!* Relax!" as if it were fine to have monsters in the church gym when it is clearly *not* fine. I guess that's when the *tremendo lloradero* happened. The way I acted that day is a running joke in our family now, and even I think it's a little funny that I was so scared of dancers.

Going to see the dances means that I have to live down my *tremendo lloradero* for the rest of my life, but I am grateful for Guadalupe and how we celebrate her. My mom always says that Gua-dalupe is *nuestra madre*—that she's everyone's mom, whoever they are in the world. Guadalupe is a tradition that's big enough to hold my family and all the people in all the states of Mexico with all their different dances. Not everyone gets to be part of something so enormous, and I love my relationship with Our Lady of Guadalupe.

5

Hunter College

Over Christmas break, I make sure Cleo practices her song a lot and I try to get her to sing louder. I think of different places and tell her: "Make sure they can hear you in Alaska!" "They have to hear you in China!" "In Mexico!" I think of a lot of faraway places. Cleo's voice is beautiful, and once, when she was practicing, I looked over at my mom and I think I saw a tear in the corner of her eye. The song is sad—Cleo plays a little girl in a detention center singing about how much she misses her home. Still, it's interesting to me that my mom has tears in her eyes, because she doesn't cry very often.

The last time I saw my mom cry, it was also because of our show. It was the big performance last year at City Hall. My mom had been to other performances before, but she had never really been able to watch. She always had Natalia and Alma with her, and they take up a lot of attention. But the day of the City Hall performance, my aunt took care of Natalia and Alma so that my mom could go to the show by herself. In the middle of the show I looked out at my mom and . . . she was crying! I almost forgot my lines I was so surprised. On the way home I kept asking my mom, "Mami, why were you *llorando*?" At first she brushed me off, but I kept asking her again and again. Finally, she told me: it was because she was so proud to see me speaking all those big lines onstage, by myself, when I used to be so shy.

I thought about it for a minute. I guess I was really shy when I was a little kid. I would hide behind my mom, like Alma does now when she's scared to talk to someone, and I was very quiet at school. I wanted to be an A+ / 100 percent student, so I was afraid of making too much noise—what if the teacher heard and I got in trouble? When I went out with my mom, I would talk to her and ask her questions about the people we passed— like, "Mami, what game do you think those kids are playing?" She would say, "¡Ve y pregunta¡" but I didn't like asking strangers questions. I guess it made my mom worry that I wouldn't speak up for myself.

I still remember the first day I walked into Still Waters and how nervous I felt looking around the room at all the kids of all different ages. I didn't know whether the teenagers would be nice ones or the kind who make fun of little kids. I didn't want my mom to leave. But I also remember that after only a few minutes, the other kids at Still Waters had me sit on the couch. Sitting on the couch is comfy-cozy, and it was really nice of everyone to let me sit there because I was new. When it was time for my first writing lesson, I remember Stephen would say things like, "Don't worry," and "There's no wrong answer." That made me worry

less about sharing my ideas. Now, the other performers from Still Waters are like my family, and I don't mind if they hear me talk. Besides, it's not really *me* who's speaking in the play: it's Kid Quixote Sarah. Even though I don't necessarily feel that I'm being so brave by saying my lines loud and clear to the audience, my heart glows thinking that I made my mom so proud by being in this show. I can't wait for her to see it when Cleo and I sing together—we will be an amazing performing-sisters duo then.

All of January, we rehearse our show with the new prisoner scene at Still Waters. I like how it feels very bright and cozy inside Still Waters, when the days outside are cold and gray. Stephen sends home permission slips for our tour during February break, and my mom signs Cleo and me up for all the shows: Columbia University, Hunter College, Drexel University, and Yale University, all in one week. Everyone is really excited. We talk about who we will sit next to on the bus and what snacks we are going to bring.

When school ends the Friday before February break, my other friends at school shout goodbye and get ready for a week of no school and nothing to do. I head straight to Still Waters after school on Friday afternoon, and again on Saturday morning so we can keep practicing, to be ready for our tour. We have performed for college students before, but never so many, and never so far away from Brooklyn. The Saturday before the show, we do a run-through of the entire performance with all the scenes and songs we have been writing together. We have been working on this show for three years, so we know it really well, but somehow everyone is too nervous and we have to keep stopping and starting again.

The other kids forget that they have to let me turn the pages of the big copy of *Don Quixote* three times before the singing begins. I forget to say "Mami, everything I do is because I love you so much in my heart" at the beginning of the show. Paulo mixes up his "Fleece Navidad" joke, so it's not funny. Then we get to the new prisoner scene and there is no way you could hear Cleo two feet away, let alone in Alaska. This rehearsal is a disaster!

Stephen stops the rehearsal, and everyone sits down in a big square. We put away our props, because sometimes the little kids get distracted and play with the flowers and puppets instead of focusing on instructions. He gives us what I call an *inspirational speech*. He tells us that he knows we are nervous about the tour, but the way to deal with being nervous is to take deep breaths. He asks us to stop thinking about everything that is happening *outside* and instead narrow in on

our imaginations, where Don Quixote's story is unfolding. We have to be totally involved in what's happening in the circle, in the performance, otherwise the audience will also be distracted. Most important, we have to project our voices *loudly* so that everyone hears us.

Even after Stephen's inspirational speech, everyone leaves rehearsal feeling a little bit nervous. What if we make the same mistakes in front of a huge audience? We are doing the performance four different times this week, and I want them all to be really good. I worry about it all day Sunday, when we are supposed to be resting, but the next thing I know, it's Monday morning and we are headed to Still Waters.

My mom is coming with us to most of the performances, so Cleo and my mom and I get to Still Waters very early on the day of the first show. We get there so early Stephen hasn't even rolled up the gate, which is painted with different people's names in bright graffiti. The first person to arrive is Monica, a grown-up who volunteers to help stage-manage our shows. She helps us with the writing when we are making new parts of the show, and she always carries a script with her if you need help with your lines. Monica has a car, so she can pack up all the props and bring them to our performances for us, which is good, because it would be pretty hard to carry it all on the subway! She talks to Cleo about the Baby-Sitters Club, which Cleo is reading, while we wait. Then Stephen gets there, rolls up the gate, unlocks the door, and we wait inside in the warm while the other kids file in.

By nine thirty in the morning, everyone has arrived except Joseph. We have to head to the subway soon or we will be late for our performance at Hunter College, but still no Joseph. Finally, we realize that we will have to leave—one of the other kids will have to play Joseph's part—and then just as we are all walking to the subway, he arrives! Everyone runs to hug him and clap him on the back because we are so happy to see him, and I completely forget to be nervous for our show.

The subway ride is a lot of fun. We go from our neighborhood in Brooklyn and across the river to Manhattan, a different part of New York City. There's a great view of the Manhattan skyline when we cross the river, and guess what? It has started snowing! We all cheer at the icy white flakes spinning down over the river, the bridge, and the skyscrapers. Then the subway goes underground and pulls into Union Square, a big station in downtown Manhattan where we switch trains. Percy is carrying a subway map, and he shows everyone that we have to get on the green 6 train to go uptown to Hunter College. While he is showing us, the other adults shout at us to stay together and keep moving with the group, so he folds up his map quickly and stuffs it into his pocket. The train uptown is more crowded, but the Still Waters gang packs inside, and the next thing we know, the conductor is announcing "Sixty-Eighth Street—Hunter College!" and we all jump out and line up on the platform.

When we make it to the top of the subway stairs, onto the street, it has started snowing for real. The ground is covered with slush, and one side of the street has been closed so that the snow plow can get through. I hope Monica will be able to get to Hunter safely in her car—the subway is mostly underground, so we didn't have to worry about the roads, but they sure look slippery.

We go into the lobby of Hunter College, which has big purple banners hanging down—their school color. There's a snack bar and a big open space where students are hanging out, reading, and studying. Some of them are talking, some of them are poring over enormous textbooks, and some of them are on their computers. They look like they are having fun. I wonder if any of them are thinking, "Today I will see an amazing performance of *The Traveling Serialized Adventures of Kid Quixote* performed by the kids of Still Waters in a Storm from Brooklyn, New York." I also wonder what it's like to be in college and study with your friends at the snack bar.

Ruth gets a call from Monica on her phone; she made it to Hunter safely but was only able to park a few blocks away, and she doesn't know which building we are in, because Hunter College has many buildings. The grown-ups send the three teenagers together to help Monica find the building and carry in all the props. While they are gone, a professor from Hunter College named Professor Diana meets us all in the lobby. She is wearing a Still Waters in a Storm T-shirt! The T-shirt has a silhouette of Don Quixote and Sancho Panza, and on the back it reads, "Everyone listens to everyone," which is our motto at Still Waters. Stephen had given it to her as a gift, and she wore it to show that she was looking forward to our performance.

Professor Diana leads us up three sets of escalators, then we walk over a long sky bridge that connects one building to another without needing to go outside. It's like a long hallway suspended between the two buildings. If you look out the window, you feel like you are flying—and we can see the snow is starting to stick down below.

The people at Hunter have already set up a big classroom for our performance. The grown-ups rearrange the chairs into the square we need for our show while we all have our lunch. There are cold cuts and sandwiches and soda, but we have to wait until after the show to have the sodas—Stephen told us a story about how once when he was in a show he decided to have a Coke, and then in the middle of the performance, just when he had his biggest line, he opened his mouth and out came a—

BURP!

So now none of us have any soda until *after* our show, because it would be very bad if that happened to us in the middle.

After lunch, Kim sets up her keyboard and we

gather around to do our warm-up exercises. After our "The lips, the teeth, the tip of the tongue" exercises, we do a posture exercise. We close our eyes and imagine that our legs and feet are like the roots of a tree trunk. We imagine that they are sinking deep, deep into the ground, growing through all the floors of Hunter College, through the sidewalk, into the subway, sinking even below the subway. The deeper the roots of your tree go, the straighter and taller you will grow. Then, it is time to begin our show.

We take our places, and the college students file in. They fill the room. I turn the pages of the book. One turn. Two turns. Three turns. The other kids sing out:

De claro en claro
de turbio en turbio
leyendo, imaginando, y creyendo

The show has begun!

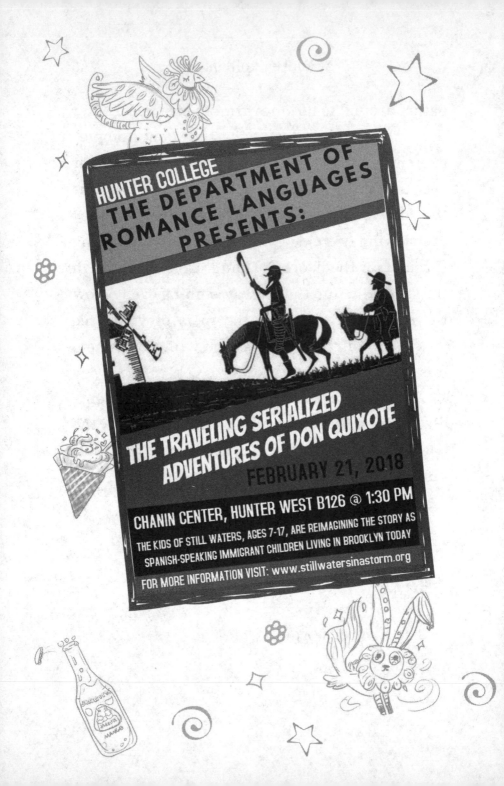

6

Cleo Sings

The performance is going well, but minutes before the prisoner scene, some kind of really loud vent picks up. It makes a *whooshing* sound that drowns out our voices. We all try to speak louder and project our voices like we practiced. But the sound is distracting, and it's almost time for Cleo's solo!

I reach the line of prisoners and begin to sing: ¿Cuál es tu nombre? *What is your name?*

I sing my question three times.

Soon it's Cleo's turn to answer.

Cleo looks small and scared, which is how she is supposed to look according to the script. She is being held prisoner, after all. My mom gave her a new haircut before the show, a cute bob that makes her look even smaller and sweeter. When I ask her the third question, "Where is your home?" that's her cue to start singing. The vent *whooshes*. Cleo opens her mouth. The *whooshing* gets louder.

But Cleo is even louder! She sings out so you can hear her over the vent, across the room, and, probably, in Alaska. I am so proud I could hug her.

She sings: *A rainbow house with a silver roof where the sun will always shine.*

I reply: *Who is your family?*

She sings: El aroma de los tamales que mama me hizo para mi

I am proud of that line because I helped write it. It means: *The smell of tamales that mom made for me.* When we were writing letters to the undocumented girls, one of them told us that the food wasn't very good. It made me sad thinking about how I can get tamales and flautas and all sorts of good food in Brooklyn, and I wished I could send them some tamales. People making good food is one of the first things I think of when I think about my family.

Now I ask: *How did you come here?*

She sings: *We followed the path of the
     singing coyote.*

This is the line where parents start crying in the audience, and I am so glad Cleo is projecting so we can be certain that my mom can hear it even if she is sitting all the way in the back. It is a heartbreaking line—a *coyote* isn't just an animal, it's also the name for people who bring immigrants from places where there is violence or terrible poverty to the United States. Some coyotes lead immigrants by walking across the desert, others run rafts across the Rio Grande on the border, others drive trucks or smuggle immigrants onto trains. Coyotes cost a lot of money, and they can be cheats—sometimes they take poor people's money and don't actually get them to the United States. When that happens, the people are worse off than they were before—they don't make it to the United States *plus* they have lost all their money. Some of the immigrants who do make it to the United States get jobs, because a lot of companies want to hire undocumented immigrants—they can get away with paying them less than citizens, and companies always need people to work. But some undocumented immigrants end up in detention centers, like the girls we have been writing to at Still Waters. In both cases, crossing the border with the coyotes is a very scary memory and makes people feel very sad—when they hear Cleo's beautiful voice singing it, they often cry.

My next question in our duet is: *Why are you alone?*

Cleo sings: *I lost my mommy's hand.*

Then I ask the most important question of all:

What do I need to know to enter your
*   fragile little heart?*

Cleo replies: *Hug me tight; tell me to close*
*   my eyes; tell me I'm safe and this is just*
*   a bad dream.*

I am ready to cry myself. I want to reach out and give Cleo a hug right then and there, and if I could I would also go to every one of the undocumented girls in the detention center and instead of a letter I would give them each an enormous hug. I would hug them for hours and hours so they would not feel sad or afraid.

The show is about to continue, but I give myself just one second to look at the audience. I see that my mom is watching us, both of her daughters, singing together. There are tears in her eyes this time too, but now I know these aren't only tears because I have been brave and bold performing onstage—they are tears because my mom understands that it's hard to be an immigrant sometimes. Even though my mom is a grown-up, maybe she still misses my abuela Beatriz, who lives all the way in Mexico. I promise myself that as soon as the play is over, I am going to give my mom an extra-enormous hug.

The music starts again, and I free the prisoners. Sancho Panza and I decide that our next stop on our epic adventure will be visiting an ancient library, and the whole cast sings the final song of this episode, the "Adventurous Adventure Song." Then we shout the last line like a punch:

To the library!

7

To the Library!

The next part of *The Traveling Serialized Adventures of Kid Quixote* will be based on a story that takes place in a library, so Stephen wants us to visit as many libraries as possible before we begin writing the library scene.

After our performance, and after all the parents hug us and the college students ask us questions, Professor Diana brings us to the library. The Hunter College library does not look like an ancient library that a knight would visit. It looks sleek and modern. That is fine, because when we write our version of Don Quixote we can always change parts of the book so that they make sense to people living today. Like the lobby of Hunter, this library is full of college students. Some of them are sitting at desks studying quietly. Some of them are huddled in groups on big padded benches, working on group projects. The library is divided into different floors, depending on whether you are working on something totally silent or whether you are working with a group and need to talk. We take the elevator from floor to floor, and it is *very* hard for some people in our group to stay quiet on the silent floors. The grown-ups have to tell them to knock it off.

The library has a lot of books, but also a lot of spaces for students to work. They have thought of a good system to fit a lot of the books in the library without taking up too much space. It's called compact shelving. Compact shelves look like regular bookshelves, except that they are very tall and go up to the ceiling and are made of metal and plastic. There is a big wheel on the end of each shelf that looks like the crank underneath an office chair. When you turn that wheel, the shelf moves easily, even with the weight of all the heavy books, because the shelf is on special wheels. When no one is using the books, all the shelves are rolled together so that there is no aisle between them. That way, they take up very little space. Then, when someone needs a book, they pick the right shelf and roll back that bookshelf to create an aisle.

The librarian tells us that there are thousands of books in the library, but they can always find the books because each book has an address, just like your apartment has an address. The book's address is its *call number*. At the end of every shelf, above the wheel crank, there is a sticker that says the range of call numbers on that shelf. If you want to find a book in the library, you look online at the card catalog, which tells you the book's call number, and then you walk up and down the compact shelving until you find the shelf with the right call numbers. Then you roll back the shelf and walk down the aisle you made to the right book address.

The compact shelving is pretty smart, and all of us have lots of ideas on how we could use it in the play. For starters, the compact shelving could be a good way for Don Quixote to trap a villain—squished between the shelves! We also love the idea of a call number being like a book's address, and the aisle being like the street where the book lives.

Later that week, we visit more libraries, at each university we go to. Some of them are very sleek and new, like the Hunter College library. Others are very quiet and old, like a library we visit at Yale University that has four *million* books. The books are so old that you can't take them home with you, and to look at the books you can't just walk up to the right compact shelf and roll it open. You have to ask for the book, then they take you to a special room where you put on white gloves. Then they bring you the book, and you can only look at the book for a few minutes in the room. The paper is so old and fragile that if they let you take the book outside it might just turn to dust and disappear. I can't wait to write the library scene!

8

My Abuela Araceli

On Sundays, we get to spend a lot of time with my dad. My siblings and I love Sundays because it's always special to spend a whole day with him. My dad is a cook and also works at a catering company, so normally he is very busy. But on Sundays, my mom goes to work and my dad takes all of us to church with him. He teaches us that faith is very important, and so we try to go to mass regularly.

Sometimes on Sundays we see our other brother (our stepbrother) Caleb, who we don't get to see that much because he works and goes to school, but when we do, we play video games or go to the park, and it makes us really happy to see him. Other times, my dad takes us to the tortillería where my abuela Araceli works. It is only a couple of blocks from our house, and it is half restaurant, half tortilla factory. Abuela gives us a *ton* of food when we visit. By the end of the afternoon, we are so stuffed we can't even look at anything else to eat. Have you ever been to a tortillería? This is what ours looks like:

On the restaurant side, there are tables and chairs and lots of people enjoying good food. There is a painting of Guadalupe on the wall, and it looks a lot like any other place you've eaten. On the factory side, there are a ton of boxes and an enormous machine the size of an entire wall. The machine takes balls of masa (dough) and flattens them with a metal press to make the tortilla shapes. Then it shoots the flattened tortillas onto a long conveyor belt so they can be packaged and sold to Mexican restaurants all over Brooklyn.

The tortillería means a lot to our family

because it is where my parents met each other. My mom had just come to the United States from Puebla, Mexico, and got a job packaging the tortillas. Whenever my dad visited the tortillería to talk to my grandmother, he would talk to my mom. Little by little, they got to know each other, and that's how our family started.

When Diego and I were born, my mom kept working at the tortillería, and when I was a toddler she would bring me to work with her, so I used to spend a lot of time at the tortillería even if I don't really remember it because I was so little. Now I go there only on Sundays, and my mom doesn't work there anymore—she is very busy most of the time with my little sisters, and on Sundays she works with my friend Talia's mom.

The tortillería smells a little like fresh flowers, and also like something else that doesn't have a name—like maybe my abuela and the other women put a magic ingredient into the tortilla masa. An ingredient that's been around a really long time—since Aztec people were the only ones in Mexico, or since ancient Egypt—I just like to

think there's something very special in that masa.

I like to use the word "masa" instead of "dough" when I talk about tortillas, because usually, in the tortillería, I am talking to someone in my family who mostly speaks Spanish—plus, I

think "masa" sounds a little bit better. When I say "masa," I remember the way the tortillería smells, and how quickly the women make the masa into balls and feed them into the machine. It's so fast it looks like a secret handshake.

When my siblings and I get tired of stuffing ourselves in the tortillería, we go next door to the apartment where tons of my cousins live. They are mostly older cousins, so we can't really play with them, but we *do* play with their pets. There is a dog named Chase, who belongs to my cousin, and a black cat named Tiger, who belongs to my abuela. Chase is a little dog with curly fur, mostly white with spots of brown. I love playing with Chase. If I had my own dog it would be a golden retriever, but I doubt my parents are getting me one anytime soon (it would be hard to fit a golden retriever in an apartment). Instead, I play with Chase and I watch the real golden retrievers through the window of the doggie daycare in my neighborhood. There are also cute little dogs at the doggie daycare, and it is one of the best places to stop and watch if you are going for a walk in Brooklyn.

Tiger is funny because you would expect him to have orange stripes like a tiger, but instead he is all black. He reminds me of the cat in the story "Puss in Boots," and he jumps so far so fast that I can practically imagine he has magic boots that let him travel a million miles.

I like to play with Chase and Tiger in the apartment next to my abuela's tortillería because we don't have any pets at my apartment except one goldfish. Our goldfish doesn't really have a name, but you should be impressed by our goldfish because it is a *survivor* fish. Last summer we won five goldfish at a fair on Myrtle Avenue. It was one of those games where you have to shoot balls into the right places, and if you get enough goals, you win goldfish. My dad got tickets for all of us (well, not Alma, because she's a baby), and we won prizes—you can't stop the Sierra siblings!

When we brought home the goldfish, my mom was a *little* worried. It turns out goldfish are actually a lot of work for such small pets. They need a tank, and the tank needs to be cleaned regularly, and you have to change the water all the time. You also have to feed the goldfish special fish food. We promised my mom we would do it, but then we kept forgetting, and the next thing we knew, four of the goldfish were dead.

Cleo felt terrible and wanted to keep the goldfish even after they died, which is impossible—they would start to stink! Still, she cried when she found out we had to flush them down the toilet. My brother, Diego, cheered her up by making a big show of holding a goldfish funeral (in the bathroom). As many of us who could fit gathered in the bathroom—even my littlest sisters and my little cousins—and Diego sang "Tan-ta-RA!" then gave a eulogy about how these four had been the best fish in the world. By then, Cleo was smiling, and all of us put our hands over our hearts and pretended the goldfish had died heroes' deaths. They sort of had—being our pets even for a week was kind of heroic!

The funny thing about the goldfish is that after four of the goldfish died, we expected the other one wouldn't be far behind—but it lived. It just kept swimming. So today we have one survivor goldfish.

After we play with the pets for a long time, our stomachs start growling, which is surprising after

that enormous lunch my abuela
gave us, but I guess we are just
hungry again. We all go back
to the tortillería to beg my dad
to take us for *crepas.*

A tornado *crepa* is a treat
that is unique to our neighborhood. Basically, it is ice cream,
crumbled Oreos, banana, whipped
cream, and chocolate sauce all wrapped up in
a crepe and served in a paper cone. It is a tornado of sugar and chocolate and ice cream, and
it is definitely the best treat in the neighborhood.
We pay at the front near the door, then we run to
the back to get a table. The tables are so funny
because someone has painted animal ears on the
wall behind each table. If you sit in front of them,
it looks like you are wearing those animal ears.
There are antlers like a deer and long floppy ears
like a bunny. So even though our apartment is a
little short on furry pets, we get to play with pets
at the tortillería—and pretend to be pets at the
crepas place!

9

The Tower of Babel

At Still Waters we are finally writing the library scene of our show. Cleo and I get there on Saturday just as Talia, who is about Cleo's age, is rolling in on her bicycle. Some of the kids are playing soccer inside. When Paulo and Bernadette arrive, my uncle is carrying a big tray of pasta with cheese and vegetables. One of the fun things about Still Waters is that all the parents take turns bringing us food and snacks for lunch. Sometimes we get pasta, or sometimes we get frijoles and rice. We know a lot of people who work at restaurants,

so the food is always extra delicious. While we
wait for everyone to arrive, Stephen serves us big
bowls.

By the time all the kids get there, Bernadette
and Wendy and I have already read about a thousand *Calvin and Hobbes* comics. Hayden, who is a
college student who volunteers at Still Waters on
Saturdays, is sitting with the teenagers. I notice
that Alex has dyed her hair blue, and I am so jeal-
ous because I love turquoise, but my mom says I'm
not old enough to dye my hair yet. Kim arrives
and gets everything set up on her keyboard, and
then Stephen calls us all over to the big tables.

There are a lot of people at Still Waters today,
so we have to get some chairs from the corner and
push an extra bench up near the table, and a few
of the little kids squeeze in together. Before we get
to the library scene, Kim has a lot to tell us. She
has been in Minnesota recording an album of her
own music that she composed—not the music for
our show, but music she has been writing all on
her own. She told us that it took a lot of tries to get
everything right for the recording—they did two

hundred and seventy takes, in fact! That is *a lot* of takes. Kim tells us all about the recording studio so we can be ready for when we go there ourselves to record the songs from our show. I hope it doesn't take us two hundred and seventy takes. By that time, the little kids would be melting down and so would I! Sometimes Stephen and Kim make us practice a scene or a line over and over again, but I don't think we have ever had to practice anything two hundred and seventy times in a row. We are all really proud of Kim for recording her own album—and a little worried about recording ours.

Now, it's time to begin writing. Stephen passes around sheets of paper from a big yellow pad. Everyone scrambles to find a pencil. When we write a new scene for our show, it usually starts with Stephen reading to us from a book or telling us a story, and all the kids write down our reactions. We use all the reactions we wrote down to brainstorm ideas for our scene. For the library scene, we have already gotten a head start because we have visited so many libraries. But first, Stephen begins with a story.

This story is called "The Tower of Babel." It is originally from the Bible, but now Stephen tells us his own version of the story. In the story, all the people on Earth speak one language, and they all understand one another. Then they decide that they want to build a tower so tall and big that it will reach heaven. The people are curious about what God is doing up there, so they keep building higher and higher. The tower becomes like its own universe, with different people living and working in different parts, and all the while the tower grows taller and taller until finally it is almost at the very tip-top of heaven. Then one day an archer climbs to the very highest part of the tower. He points his bow and arrow, pulls back the bow, and *pow!* His arrow pierces a cloud.

By now, God is furious at the people. You can't get to heaven by climbing or by shooting bows and arrows. You have to earn heaven, and you have to believe in it to get there. By building the tower, the people had been acting like show-offs, as if they were more powerful than God. So God decided to punish the people by making them all speak different languages. The different languages made it harder for them to understand one another, and they decided to stop building the tower and scatter far and wide. Some people say that's why there are so many different languages around the world today—because of the Tower of Babel.

After Stephen finishes the story, we all look around at one another. It was a pretty good story, but how can we use it in our play? Then Stephen tells us something else—to imagine that the tower was like a universe, and that each of the people working on building the tower was like a book. He tells us that some people think that each human is like a book, and that each book is like a human. That changes things—now we can imagine the tower as an enormous library, as big as the universe.

There's one more story Stephen wants to read

us before we begin writing, and that's a story by
a man named Jorge Luis Borges. It's from a book
of short stories called *Ficciones*. One of the stories is called "The Library of Babel" and begins
with the words *El universo, (que otros llaman la
Biblioteca)*"—"The universe, which others call
the library." In this library, bulbs of fruit hang
from the ceiling and give off a glowing light. It's
exactly like what we were just talking about—if
every book is a human and every human is a book,
then maybe the library is like a universe-worth of
humans. Maybe the library holds everything you
could ever want to know about people, because
each book *is* a person. Percy raises his hand and
says that maybe every aisle in the library is like a
galaxy, and the whole building together is the universe. I like that idea, and especially the idea that
every book lives at an address—a call number—
just like people live at addresses where you can
find them, too.

We pick up our pencils, and it's time to begin
the brainstorming process. Stephen instructs us
to write about the universe, and libraries. We can

write anything we think of—a story or a poem, or we can make a long list of everything we associate with the library, and the universe. Sometimes when you are stuck writing, making a list like that can help you get ideas without feeling too stressed.

Stephen takes his phone out of his pocket, and Joseph and Percy and Santiago cheer. "It's the duck timer!" Percy says.

"That's right," Stephen says. "It's back!" He taps the screen, and we hear a loud sound that is a cross between a *quack!* and a *honk!* It sounds exactly like a duck, and everyone giggles. Stephen sets the timer and places his phone down in the center of the table. When we have had ten minutes to write, the duck timer will make its *quack!/ honk!* sound, and we will know it's time to stop writing. In the meantime, everyone should be working silently at the table.

I drum my fingers on the edge of the table. I am trying to think of something really interesting to say about the universe. I know that Earth is in the universe, and so we all live inside the universe,

but when I think of the universe I don't actually
think about Earth. Instead, I
think about outer space,
about stars and planets
and galaxies beyond
the Milky Way. I write
far away, starry, and
planets on my paper.
I doodle a little unicorn in
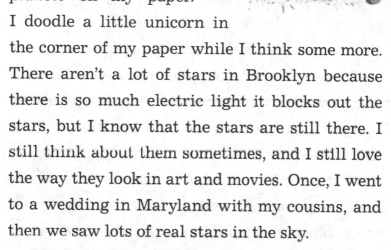
the corner of my paper while I think some more.
There aren't a lot of stars in Brooklyn because
there is so much electric light it blocks out the
stars, but I know that the stars are still there. I
still think about them sometimes, and I still love
the way they look in art and movies. Once, I went
to a wedding in Maryland with my cousins, and
then we saw lots of real stars in the sky.

My dad and I watch a lot of old movies together,
and there is a lot in those movies that makes me
think of the universe—of traveling through time
and space. *Time Bandits* is one of those movies,
and so are *Back to the Future* and *E.T.,* so I write
all of those down on my paper as well. Then I

have another good idea. Earlier, I heard Stephen mention something about how the ocean is almost like its own galaxy because it is so vast and dark and deep. Those words "dark" and "vast" make me think about black holes, which are places in outer space where there is no light at all, just pure darkness, no color at all. We learned in school that scientists just this year took the very first picture of a black hole. Because how can you get a picture of something that isn't really a *thing*, it's a *nothing*—no light at all, just darkness? The scientists figured out how to take pictures of all the light around the black hole so you could see the darkness at the center. When I saw that picture, it made me think a little bit of the heart of a whirlpool. Have you ever swirled your finger in a circle really hard in the bathtub, again and again until it makes a whirlpool? I think if you look down into the very center of the whirlpool, it is almost like that picture of a black hole. I write *whirlpool/ black hole* on my paper.

"QUACK! HONK!"

Everyone laughs as we put down our pencils.

Some people's hands shoot straight up, including mine. I think some of my ideas could be interesting for our show, even though I don't know exactly how we could use them. But Stephen tells us we don't have to raise our hands. Instead, everyone will go one by one based on when they feel like speaking. I think I've told you that the most important rule at Still Waters is "Everyone listens to everyone," and this is when that rule is most important. You have to listen to all the other people reading their ideas before it's your turn to share your ideas, and *everyone* at the table participates. Even the grown-ups: Stephen, Kim, Monica, Hayden—they all share their writing with us too. We printed "Everyone listens to everyone," on the back of the T-shirts because it is such an important motto for our program.

A lot of people have great ideas. Ruth, one of the teenagers, has the idea that just like most of the universe hasn't been explored yet and we are still learning to understand the universe, maybe we are also still learning to understand ourselves—especially us kids and teenagers. Then someone else adds that it's as if our books are still being written, and our library is still growing and expanding. Just like the compact shelves at the Hunter College library can grow and expand to add more books to the collection, as humans learn more and write more, our library will grow.

Cleo and I leave Still Waters full of new ideas about the universe and the planets and the stars. We can't wait to get home and tell our parents about it, and maybe watch some more old movies about the universe with my dad. I have a tingling feeling all over, and it tells me that this library scene is going to be a good one.

10

My Father

Not everyone knows that my dad is an artist. He can draw or paint or sculpt almost anything. When he does his job at the catering company, he sometimes makes sculptures out of the food to display at the event—until the hungry guests gobble them up! He can make sculptures from chocolate, from fruit, or from sugar. Not a lot of people know how to do that, and my dad's creations make these events extra special. I know that if someone showed up at one of my Still Waters performances with a chocolate sculpture, I would be extremely impressed.

I have learned a few things about art from my dad. He tells me stories about some of the jobs he had before he worked as a cook and a caterer. When I was very young, he worked at a mannequin factory in Manhattan. A mannequin is like a statue of a model that stores use to display how the clothing would work on real people—you have probably seen mannequins in store windows. Some mannequins are very simple and don't have many details, while other mannequins are elaborate and they look almost like real people. Mannequins are very challenging to make, and sometimes it takes a whole month to do just one. When my dad worked at a mannequin factory, he would pour the fiberglass resin into molds the shape of people, then help assemble, sand, and paint the mannequin. He liked that job because it was sculpture and painting rolled into one. It required a lot of detail and skill. When the company moved to France, my dad got a different job, but he still does art whenever he can.

My dad helps us with the artwork at Still Waters. Once, for an end-of-the-year performance, he drew a silhouette of Don Quixote on the balloons and even on the cake we had at our celebration. In case you have never seen what a silhouette of Don Quixote looks like, it is an outline of an old tall knight (Don Quixote) next to his short sidekick (Sancho Panza) and a slow skinny horse (Rocinante). In the background there is a windmill, and everyone who sees that silhouette knows right away that it is supposed to represent Don Quixote. That is because in the book, Don Quixote gets confused and thinks that a windmill is a giant. He attacks the windmill because he is convinced that it is a giant who will harm Dulcinea if he does not tame it.

In our show, one of the teenagers, Joshua, plays Professor Windmill, who explains the meaning of the windmills. He tells the audience that the arms of the windmill, spinning round and round to capture the energy in the wind, represent "the relentless turning of the mind"—what happens when you start thinking about something and you

can't stop, you just keep thinking about it over and over again until you start to get worried and scared and imagine that there's a monster under your bed—or that a windmill *is* a monster. When I think about "the windmill of the mind" I think about a clock striking the same hour again and again, or how the wheel of fortune turns in a circle. I also think about when you bang your head in a cartoon and little birds circle around your head, because when the windmill in your mind is turning around and around, it doesn't feel so great.

Every human being knows the feeling of thinking about something so much that you have convinced yourself it is something terrible and scary, which is why the audience laughs when Don Quixote attacks a windmill, but secretly, they all understand—we all know what it's like to overthink something. We would all love to be able to attack the thoughts that keep us from sleeping, keep us worried all the time. That's how I feel when I think about the migrant girls who are being held in the detention center—I would like

to stop thinking about it, but I can't, and I would like to be able to rescue them, but I can't. I understand why Don Quixote went after the windmill.

I love my dad's drawings of Don Quixote, Sancho Panza, Rocinante, and the windmill just like I loved wearing my Frida costume to school for Hispanic Heritage Month—I feel like I have a little piece of my dad with me when I see his drawings. When I see my dad's drawings, I don't have to worry about bad thoughts turning over and over in my mind—the windmill in my  brain is calm and peaceful. One day soon, he is going to repaint the metal gate that covers Still Waters when Stephen closes it up at night. Right now it has lots of graffiti names on it, but my dad is going to turn it into an awesome mural when he has time this summer.

My dad also helps me make my own art and paintings some of the time. For example, in April it will be the state exams, which are a big deal in my school. The teachers want us to feel excited and confident the day of the exam, so the whole school wears matching T-shirts that day. The shirts always have something encouraging on them, like "We will *slam* this exam!" and every year there is a competition to see who can design the best T-shirt.

This year, I decide I want to enter the competition. I want to make a shirt that has our school mascot, an eagle, and a motto around the eagle in a circle. The motto will be: "Knowledge is the strength of life," which is something my dad says all the time. I think those would be the perfect words for the exam.

I ask my dad for help because I'm not sure I can draw a good eagle on my own. We sit down at the kitchen table while my mom is putting the little kids to sleep, and my dad has me draw several circles on a piece of paper. We will erase the circles later, but for now it is a good guide so that our eagle will be proportional. I do my best to draw his beak and feathers, and then my dad points out to me how I have clumped all the feathers in one part of the grid—I need to stretch them out so that they cover the whole area. My dad helps me redraw them in pencil. After a lot of erasing and moving parts, it's finally time to go over our lines in ink. My dad gets me a Sharpie, and I trace our pencil lines—only the body of the eagle, of course. When the ink is dry, we erase the pencil circles and blow away the rubber bits left by the eraser. It looks *amazing*. I can't wait to show my teachers.

I bring my drawing into school on Monday to show my classroom teachers, Ms. Ajayi and Ms. Markovic. The night before, my dad helped me pack the drawing neatly into a folder and slide the folder into my backpack so it wouldn't get squished. He leaves early in the morning for work, and it's my mom and all five of us during the morning rush to get to school. Here is how we get to school each day: my mom walks Diego, Cleo, and me to the bus stop. I race Cleo to see who can get there fastest, and we leave everyone else in the dust. Diego is in middle school, so his bus comes first, and we all wave goodbye to him. Then the school bus for Cleo and me arrives, and we ride together. My mom takes Natalia to preschool herself, and Alma is too little for school, so she stays with my mom all day.

Ms. Warley, our principal, greets all the kindergarteners, first, and second graders as they walk into the building. The third and fourth graders go through a different door. Sometimes I stop by Cleo's door to say hello though, because I like seeing Ms. Lovato, who is the dean of kindergarten through second grade. Ms. Lovato speaks English and Spanish, so all the parents can talk to her. My mom doesn't usually come to school with Cleo and me, but when she does, I like hearing her and Ms. Lovato talk together. (Ms. Warley speaks some Spanish, like Stephen—like a little tiny bit—but Ms. Lovato can speak Spanish all the way.)

After saying hi to Ms. Lovato, we go have breakfast in the lunchroom. There are lots of things to choose from, but none of it is home-fresh, so it's not as good as the food my parents make. Still, today is a pancake day, and I like those even if they aren't home-fresh.

I say goodbye to Cleo after breakfast, and we each go to our separate classrooms. Mine is on the third floor of the school. There are many, many stairs in our school. That's actually something unique about New York City that you might not know—the schools are in buildings with many, many floors, and it's not that easy to fit a ton of kids in elevators, so everyone goes up and down stairs. Our teachers all say they are getting a workout, but us kids really don't mind it.

Ms. Ajayi and Ms. Markovic are very impressed by my drawing. Working with my dad really paid off, and my eagle looks realistic and fierce, which is exactly the kind of look you want for test day. I look at some of the drawings other kids are submitting for the competition, and I think I have a pretty good chance. We hand our drawings in to Ms. Ajayi, who will enter them into the competition with all the other drawings from around the whole school.

I sit down next to my friend Gabriela. She has her head in her hands.

"What's wrong, Gabby?" I ask.

"I feel nauseous," she says. "I'm auditioning to be in a singing performance this weekend, and I know I will be terrible."

I am surprised that Gabby thinks that, because her voice is really good. It actually reminds me of Wendy's voice when she sings. I tell her not to be nervous.

Gabby shakes her head miserably. "I can't stop thinking about it. This weekend I couldn't focus on my homework at all—every time I looked up all I could think about was how I am going to have my audition and be terrible and everyone will think I am a terrible singer."

I see. Gabby can't stop thinking about something that makes her nervous—the windmill in her mind is turning a bad thought over and over until it makes her feel miserable. She needs to stop the windmill.

I think of how much Gabby's voice reminds me of Wendy's voice, and how funny it is that my best friend at Still Waters and my best friend at

school have such similar voices. Then I think of
the scene in our show at Still Waters where I, Kid
Quixote, attack the windmill. It's because a bad
thought has been turning over in my mind again
and again so much that I become convinced that
the windmill is a giant that needs to be stopped.
I finally recover because Wendy—playing Sancho Panza, of course—helps me. She tries to stop
me from attacking the windmill, but I don't listen, so we crash into each other, then fall to the
floor. But eventually Wendy calms me down and
we sing a song together. Even though the play is
fictional, I always feel warm and relieved when
Wendy and I start singing the song. If I ever had
a bad thought turning over and over in my mind
for real, I would want a friend like Wendy to try
to stop me from attacking the windmill and to
stay with me until I calmed down. I look back at
my friend Gabby.

"Gabby," I say, "I know you're nervous. But
I have an idea—every time you think about how
nervous you are, even if it's in the middle of the

school day, look over at me. I'll see you and know that you are thinking about that audition. Then I'll think back what a great singer you are, and you'll *know* that I'm thinking that, so it will replace the nervousness at least for a little while. Okay?"

Gabby laughs a little bit. "I guess I could try that."

I hold my hand out and we high-five just as Ms. Ajayi and Ms. Markovic call for our attention.

At lunchtime, I sit next to Gabby in case she feels scared or nervous again. I am not even thinking about the drawing competition because we're having such a good time eating together, when one of the school deans comes into the lunchroom and gets everyone's attention. The next thing I know, the dean is announcing the winners of the school T-shirt competition—and I am one of them! My design will be on the front of the school T-shirt, and my friend Niya's design will be on the back. We laugh and hug, and I can't wait to get home and tell my dad!

I tell my dad about the T-shirt competition, and also about how Gabby felt scared and what I did to help her calm down. Today was like being a real-life Kid Quixote—I was a little bit of a hero because I won the T-shirt competition, and I also helped someone—no windmill attacking involved.

11

My Abuela Beatriz

Every once in a while, my abuela Beatriz, who is my mom's mom, comes to visit us from Puebla, Mexico. She isn't able to come very often, but when she does she stays for a few weeks at a time. It's very expensive to travel from Mexico to Brooklyn, so it doesn't make sense to only come for a few days. When my abuela Beatriz visits, it is kind of a big deal. I have two grandmothers, but because we see Abuela Araceli like every Sunday it's not really *news* when she is around. But when my abuela Beatriz visits, we clean the apartment, and my mother makes fresh tamales to welcome her. My uncles try to spend more time at home so they can see her often, and the little kids try to behave really well.

My mom's whole side of the family spends a lot of time together when my abuela Beatriz visits. You already know my cousins Bernadette and Paulo, but on my mom's side I also have Bruno, Aldo, and Lucas, who are a little younger than me. Everyone is really close. If one of my uncles is getting *paletas* for his kids, he gets *paletas* for every single one of us. We are ten cousins and we all share together. When my abuela Beatriz comes to visit, she spends a lot of time cooking for everyone. She is old and doesn't like to go out that often. Instead, she spends hours making us dishes like eggs with tortillas. I help her wash the dishes. Dishwashing is the best chore, I think, because it's splashy and bubbly and you can think or talk while you do it.

While we are cooking and dishwashing, my abuela Beatriz tells us all stories about Mexico. It is very different from Brooklyn. For one thing, the part of Mexico where my mom is from is very rural. There are no tall buildings and very few paved roads or cars. Instead, there is dirt and fields as far as you can see. My mom told us that when she was a kid she knew tons of people who rode horses—it was the easiest way to get around where she was from. There were a lot of other animals where my mom grew up in Mexico too, including snakes and bugs.

Once, my mom and my uncles took us all to a cabin on Bear Mountain, across the Hudson River, on the other side of New York City. There was dirt on the floor of the cabin, and you could see bugs crawling in the ground. It was quiet outside, and you could hear the wind. We wondered if a real bear would come up to our cabin, because the place was called Bear Mountain, after all. Once, the door slammed and we all shrieked and screamed, and my mom laughed at us. She couldn't believe we were so scared of nature—where she grew up there were bugs and animals everywhere. But in New York City, there aren't so many creatures. We see squirrels sitting on the stoops of the buildings and we all shout "Squirrel!" when we do, and I always peek in the windows at doggie day cares. When we go to the Laundromat, Diego and I like to crouch down and look at the ants that live in a big crack in the sidewalk nearby. It tickles a little bit if an ant crawls up your leg. But other than squirrels, dogs, and ants (and pigeons, of course—there are a lot of pigeons in New York City), we don't really have bugs or animals in Brooklyn, so thinking about the bears on Bear Mountain was scary!

My abuela Beatriz tells us lots of other stories about Mexico. She tells us stories about snakes slithering through the grass, and I find out that

in addition to the human coyotes who cross the border, there are also animal coyotes who can attack farm animals and sometimes humans. You can hear them howling at night, like in the movies.

In the evenings when everyone is going to bed,

my dad and I talk about the stories she tells me. Even though my dad's family is technically from the same state in Mexico as my mom's family, Puebla is a very large state, and my dad's family doesn't live that near my mom's family. My dad tells me that there *are* snakes and coyotes, but he also tells me lots of beautiful stories about Mexico. He has been to visit Mexico many times, and I think he knows almost as much about it as my grandmother. He tells me about the houses, and how they are not all painted either white or brown or gray or brick like in New York. Instead, people in Mexico use every color of the rainbow. The colors of the houses are bright and vibrant: sunny yellow, sky blue, bubblegum pink, and even my favorite color, turquoise. I imagine that if you walk down a street in Mexico, it would be like seeing the mane of a unicorn painted onto the houses. When my dad tells the stories, I wish I could visit Mexico with him someday.

The next day, my cousins and I are all playing in the kitchen while my abuela Beatriz is cooking again. Today she tells us the story of La Llorona.

Do you know about La Llorona? A long time before there was the movie, Mexican people told the story of La Llorona. She is a terrifying spirit. If you have never seen her, do not look her up unless you have nerves of steel. La Llorona looks like someone from the movie *Scream*. She has a long pale face, with black circles around her eyes. She is crying (that's why they call her "La Llorona"), leaving streaks across her face. She wears a ragged wedding dress that looks like it came out of a basement. La Llorona is crying because her children drowned when she was supposed to be watching them. Now she has to roam the land at night, looking for the spirits of her drowned children. The problem is, she can't tell whether kids are her own or not, so she ends up capturing other people's kids, especially children who are bad. Once, my grandmother tells us in a hushed voice, a group of kids went trick-or-treating on Halloween, and they disappeared—the mother shouted and begged, "Where are my kids" and called the police, but still, La Llorona did not free them. Instead, she gobbled up the kids to feed herself.

At the exact moment when La Llorona is gobbling up the children, my mother walks in the door carrying Alma, who is crying. My grandmother's storytelling spell is broken by the jingle of my mother's keys and Alma's wails, which sound nothing like a terrifying spirit, just regular baby crying. All of us cousins turn to my mom wide-eyed and say nothing.

"*¿Y ustedes porque me miran así?*" my mom asks, confused.

Everyone is silent. The trance of my grandmother's story lingers, making us all quiet. We think slowly.

Finally, Diego says, "Abuela just told us the story of La Llorona," and gulps down a big swallow of air.

"Mami!" my mom protests. She wags her finger at my abuela Beatriz. "*¡No los asustes!*"

She might not want my grandmother to scare us, but I think the damage is

done. I am never leaving my mother's *sight* again, because I do *not* want to be gobbled up by La Llorona.

That night, I can't stop thinking about La Llorona. I curl up close to Cleo and try to match my breath to her deep-sleeping breaths, but my heart beats fast anyway. It's like the windmill in my mind is going on overtime, turning too fast for me to keep up with it. La Llorona has turned the windmill into a giant. I keep thinking about kids being separated from their parents. La Llorona got separated from her children because they drowned. My mom got separated from her mom because she had to move to the United States to get a job and be safe, and her mother stayed behind. At least they get to see each other, but not that often. I would hate it if I had to go so long without seeing my mom.

The windmill in my mind turns to the Guatemalan girls in the ICE detention center. I think about the last letter I got from Dolores. Sometimes, when one of the kids has been writing back and forth with one girl for a long time, suddenly the next time we get a batch of letters that girl hasn't written back. Someone else writes back instead. We never find out what happened to that girl—maybe she got out of detention and found a good place to work, or maybe she got sent back to Guatemala. No one can tell us. I hope that Dolores gets out and can stay in the United States, and I hope she never stops writing me letters.

The windmill keeps spinning, and I think about all the stories I have heard about detention centers. Everyone calls the Immigration and Customs Enforcement people "ICE" because of the letters (*I-C-E*), but I know lots of Mexican people who call ICE detention centers *hieleras*—"iceboxes"— because they turn on the air-conditioning so high and don't give the people any blankets. I do not like thinking about Dolores being alone and cold with no blanket, so I huddle even closer to Cleo.

I just know that it isn't right to separate a family. Parents belong with children. It's like when you buy a new picture frame and there is a photo inside of a perfect family—two parents and two kids, one a boy and one a girl. The parents have long flowing hair, and the kids have straight shiny teeth. But the photo is only beautiful because everyone is together, held in one frame. If you cut the picture in half, it wouldn't matter how beautiful all the people were, they would still be separated, and it would be sad. That is what the ICE people are doing when they put girls in detention centers or put up a wall that makes it hard for people to visit Mexico even if their moms are there—they are ripping apart a family portrait. No one could say that is right. It's like the whole world is a bully, and Mexico and Central America are the targets of the bullying.

Cleo sighs in her sleep, and then I remember something Stephen told us when we were working on the scene where Kid Quixote rescues the farmworker from the cruel master. He told us that you can't respect the power of bullies. Instead, you should make the audience see that the bully is ridiculous. When the audience sees that, the bully loses his power. That's why in that scene we make fun of Stephen's Spanish—because Stephen plays the cruel master, and we can't respect his authority when he is nasty. Normally, we are nice about Stephen having an accent in Spanish, but we are *not* nice about it when he is acting the part of a cruel person, because we don't want anyone to think that his cruelty is okay.

I wonder how I can make the ICE people ridiculous. Even if they don't know me, I want to find some way of proving that I don't think their bullying is okay. I know! I will imagine that the ICE agents are actual ice cubes. I close my eyes and imagine them. They are ICE cubes with no eyes, because if they had eyes they would see the suffering they cause by separating parents from their kids. Then I imagine what the ICE people would wear—underwear! They would wear underwear and nothing else. I laugh out loud, then cover my mouth so that I don't wake up Cleo. If I were really a knight on an adventure, I could find magic powers that would allow me to melt the ICE cubes. Then I would find the girls, bring them tamales and sandwiches, and hug them for hours and hours. I turn over, and I am smiling a little bit. Tomorrow at Still Waters I will tell Stephen what I imagined. Maybe I'll even draw a picture of it in my copy of *Don Quixote*, so it will be recorded forever that these ICE agents are nothing but frigid eyeless ice cubes in underwear.

12

My Tiger

It's not until the following Saturday that I get a chance to tell Stephen about my ICE people idea. Actually, before I tell him about it I doodle it in my *Don Quixote* book while everyone is brainstorming for the library scene. We each have a copy of *Don Quixote* that we use for writing our play, and we are allowed to write in them. Once, I brought my copy into school, and no one in my class could believe that I was reading it. The book is so long that it is actually two separate volumes usually. When it is in one volume it is so huge and heavy, you could use it as a doorstop. I bet it would be a pretty good booster seat for Natalia and Alma. That's how big it is. It makes me feel strong and intelligent that I have been able to translate this big heavy book into a play that kids will understand. A lot of people don't read *Don Quixote* until they get to college, but at Still Waters we read it in elementary school!

When we have a break, most of the other kids go to play soccer or read *Calvin and Hobbes*. The little kids like to write and play under the tables when there is a break, I don't know why. They play a game where they try to grab Stephen's ankles from under the tables. Maybe it's because when they do grab his ankles he says, "Those raccoons! I try to stop them but they always get in!"

The little kids laugh like hyenas, so it's pretty obvious that it's them under the tables and not real raccoons, but Stephen stays in character.

"Drat! I thought I raccoon-proofed this whole building but they won't go away! *Oh no!*" He shrieks as if a real raccoon had actually gotten him, and the little kids laugh more and more.

Finally, Kim passes coloring supplies and paper under the table, which solves Stephen's raccoon problem. He comes and sits down next to me. "What are you drawing?" he asks me.

I show him my ICE person.

"Is that an ice cube?"

I nod.

"Who is it supposed to represent?"

"The ICE people."

"Why haven't you drawn any eyes?"

"Because they don't *have* eyes. Otherwise they would see how mean they are to children."

Stephen nods, and I begin to tell him

my entire story idea. How the ICE people should be wearing only underwear so that they will be ridiculous and kids won't be afraid of them. I tell him how I think the ICE people live in a giant refrigerator under the desert and how maybe they keep kids trapped down there, but if I were *really* a hero like Don Quixote we could go and rescue them.

"What would you do if you did rescue them?" Stephen asks me.

"Give them a long hug."

"For how long?"

"Hmmm . . . about three hours," I reply.

"That's a very long hug," Stephen says.

"The kids deserve it. Until they can get their parents back, I would want to give them long hugs."

Stephen takes my book from me and examines my drawing carefully. "This is a very good drawing, Sarah."

I smile a little bit. I am not as good at drawing as my dad or my brother, Diego, who loves to draw and paint with my dad, but I like to think that I got at least some of my dad's drawing talent.

"Would the tiger be a part of this story?"

I look up at Stephen. He and the other kids at Still Waters are the only people who know about the tiger. I have never told any of the kids at school about the tiger, but I told the people at Still Waters the whole story a few years ago when I was just a little kid and had just started coming to Still Waters. We were writing the very first scenes of *The Traveling Serialized Adventures of Kid Quixote* then.

When I was six or seven, I really believed the tiger story. It's a story my mom told me about how she got to the United States. She told me that a tiger had helped her travel from Mexico to the United States. See, when my mom was little, things in her house weren't so good. Her family was very poor, and they didn't have enough to eat, or clean water to drink and bathe in. To escape, my mom told me she had ridden on the back of the tiger and it had helped her cross the desert quickly, because tigers are lightning fast. When she was scared, the tiger told her to keep going. When she got to a towering wall—as tall as the Tower of Babel— that separated Mexico from the United States, she urged the tiger to jump over it. The tiger squatted low, low, lower and then—pounce! It leaped over the wall, and my mom was in the United States.

Then she said goodbye to the tiger and drove all the way from the border of Mexico to Brooklyn, in New York City, where she met my dad and had me and my brother and sisters.

After I told that story at Still Waters, one of the teenagers asked me a question. Her name was Lily, but she doesn't come to Still Waters anymore because she goes to college, and her college is not that nearby, so she lives in a dorm with a roommate. Lily patted me on the back after I told the story and asked, "Sarah, what language did the tiger speak?"

I thought that was a silly question, because obviously my mom didn't speak English when she was a kid in Mexico. *Nobody's* parents spoke English when they were kids in Mexico. So of course the tiger would have spoken to my mom in Spanish. I told Lily, and she nodded. I noticed Lily watching me a lot the whole rest of that day, but I didn't know why. Lily and the other teenagers at Still Waters are like my big sisters, so I don't mind much if they watch me.

Now that I am older, I realize why Lily was

looking at me like that. It's because tigers can't talk at all, in English, Spanish, or Nahuatl. They also can't jump over border walls, and you can't ride the back of a tiger. It made sense to me that you would be able to—after all, you can ride horses in real life.

I learned that my mom told me that story because when I was little, the real story of how she got to the United States was too sad to tell me. In real life, my mom walked and took trucks across the desert with her family. Some of the people who crossed the desert with her died. When she tells the story she still gets very sad, and she didn't think it was a very good story to tell a little kid, so instead she told me the story of the tiger. Now we tell Natalia and Alma the tiger story, until they are old enough to know the true story.

When I think of the tiger story I am sad. I wish there were a way for families to be together that wasn't so dangerous. Sometimes I imagine myself stretching, stretching, stretching, from Brooklyn to Puebla, which is a very far distance, and I wish

I did have a real-life tiger. I wish I could be little enough to believe the tiger story, like Natalia and Alma.

"You know," Stephen tells me that day, "even if you are too old to still believe in the tiger in real life, there's no reason you can't believe the tiger in your imagination. After all, the ice-cube ICE people are a part of your imagination, right? What would you do if you had the tiger with you when you were facing the ICE people?"

Stephen and I begin writing a story together, about how the tiger and I make a hole in the desert that takes us to the ICE people's refrigerator. First we bring suitcases full of blankets for the kids. Then, since the tiger can jump great distances, he and I work together to free the children and bring them back to their parents one by one. The tiger becomes like Rocinante, who Don Quixote rode around on to rescue people. I wonder if the tiger will ever be in *The Traveling Serialized Adventures of Don Quixote.*

13

Easter

My dad is off from work on Easter Sunday, and he plans a day of adventures for me and my siblings. First, we get up in the morning and get dressed up. Cleo puts on a pink floral dress, and I pick out my black pants with sparkly rhinestones on them and a blouse. Then all five of us head out to my dad. Instead of going to our regular park, where there is a playground and an asphalt skating area, we go to a park that is a little farther away. It's kind of a long walk with Natalia and Alma, but my dad wants to go to a park with a garden for our Easter celebration.

When we finally reach the park, I'm glad we walked all this way. The park is full of blooming tulips and daffodils, like something out of a picture book. There are yellow dandelions and caterpillars crawling in the grass. Finally, it's time for my dad to hide the Easter eggs. He makes us all face away and count to two hundred (he is hiding forty eggs, so he needs some time). Diego and Cleo and I entertain Alma and Natalia while we face the trunk of a big tree, trying to keep them from turning around and chasing after my dad, which would ruin the surprise.

"*¡Listo!*" my dad shouts, and it's time to start chasing after the eggs. We give Alma and Natalia a head start, and then the rest of us join the race. Diego leaps ahead of Cleo and me, dashing every direction, trying to find the eggs. He looks a little like a wild goose, which makes me burst into giggles. Diego grins and keeps jumping, making me laugh harder and harder. But I have to find the

Easter eggs! I zoom ahead of him, still giggling as I run.

There are eggs hidden behind the tulips, eggs hidden in the branches of trees, and some just lying on the grass. We leave those for Natalia and Alma, since they are too young to find the eggs that are better hidden. It takes a long time to find them all. Last year my dad hid more eggs, but it took us less time to find them because he didn't hide them as well. This year it takes us a longer time. When we finally have every single one, we sit down on the grass, open up each plastic egg, and compare our candy hauls.

After our egg hunt, it's time for church. We go after the mass to say prayers and light candles for the saints. My family often goes to different churches, because my dad has a lot of faith. Usually, we go to this church, which is only a few blocks from our house. It has stained glass and statues of Mary and Joseph. My dad has also taken us to see St. Patrick's Cathedral in Manhattan, which is the biggest Catholic church in all of New

York City. Once, we went to a Pentecostal church for my great-great-grandfather's ninety-eighth birthday, because my dad's family is Pentecostal. My dad used to be Pentecostal when he was a little baby, but after his dad died and his mom was bringing him up all by herself, he became Catholic like her. The Pentecostal church we went to for my great-great-grandfather's birthday had pink walls.

Our local Catholic church has the type of candles where you push a button and the candle goes on. Cleo and I like visiting other churches with my dad because at some churches, instead of a push button there are real candles, and you can light them with a long match blazing with fire. It's exciting, a little dangerous, and it feels somehow more real, like a better way to get God's attention for a prayer. But since today is Easter, we still want to say prayers at our church with the push-button candles. My dad gives us all quarters, and we leave them in the offertory box, push the candle buttons, and kneel down in front of Mary to say our prayers. It is quiet and peaceful in the

church. I pray for the saints, for my mom, and for all the kids in detention centers.

On the way home from church, we pass a street corner blocked off by police tape. It reads, CAUTION, in bright yellow letters. Cleo and Diego and I look at each other. We know why the tape is there—two nights ago, there was a shooting on that corner. It was only a few blocks from our apartment, near a bar. My dad woke up first and heard the gunshots and the people shouting. When Cleo and I woke up, we didn't know what was happening; we just heard so many loud noises. We turned on the TV and found out more from the news channel. My dad told us not to worry and that we are safe in our home, but Cleo and Diego and I still hurry past that spot. I try to make sure Alma and Natalia don't see it because I don't want them to feel nervous.

At our school we have lockdown drills where we have to practice shelter in place, in case anything bad—like a shooting—happens outside. When there is a lockdown drill, you have to sit in the back of the room and be very quiet. The teachers turn off the lights and close and lock the doors. I don't mind so much when there are lockdown drills because I can let my mind wander. I can think about performing in Kid Quixote, or about where Dolores, my pen pal from Still Waters, is right now. It's nice to be in school and not have to work so hard to pay attention to the teachers for a little while. The only thing that scares me is when I'm in the bathroom at school, and I'm far away from my classroom. If you are in the bathroom when a lockdown drill starts, you have to run into the nearest classroom, and it might not be with your friends or with a teacher you know very well. It could be a kindergarten classroom; it's just whichever classroom you happen to be closest to. I don't like the idea of being caught out in the hallway alone when a lockdown starts, so I always try to go to the bathroom extra quick and get back to my classroom as soon as I can.

I should have added another prayer at church. The next time my dad takes us to church, I want to light a candle for peace. I think if we just had peace that would be beautiful. No one would have to be on lockdown ever. No lockdowns at home, and no lockdowns at school. Everyone could move freely and go wherever they needed to go. You wouldn't need to ride on the back of a tiger to get around, because you would be free. I say a prayer in my head right then and there as we are walking home, but I promise myself that the next time I am at a church that has the real candles with the long matches, I will pray for peace, and for there to be no more shooters.

Alma and Natalia are tired by the time we get back to our apartment. Even Cleo is drooping. At home, my mom has just gotten back from work, and she puts on the movie *Hop* for us, which is about the Easter Bunny. While we watch it, Alma and Natalia both fall asleep. I might have had a little nap too. Chasing after eggs, eating candy, and going to church made me sleepy! In the evening, my dad brings us Domino's pizza, which my siblings and I practically inhale. My mom jokes that you wouldn't think we had just eaten all that Easter candy! It was a great Easter.

14

The Universe

Stephen keeps reading us Jorge Luis Borges's story "The Library of Babel," and we keep talking about how the universe could be like a library and each person could be like a book. We talk about how it relates to the scene we are writing for our show. Someone says that if we think of the library like a universe, each of the books could be like a star or a planet where you have an adventure. But it's hard to figure out how to connect all the dots when we haven't even started writing!

While we are talking, a friend of Stephen's

comes in the door. He introduces himself as Jeremy Tinker and tells us that he is a professor of space science. He thinks if we learn more about the universe in the real world, we might have more ideas for the episode we are trying to write in our play. The professor tells us a lot of things you might not know about the stars. He tells us that stars are really burning and that they are superhot, hotter than you can imagine. We learn that the light

from stars takes many years to reach all the way to Earth, and when you do go out somewhere in the country where you can see the stars, you are really seeing starlight from a very long time ago—before you or your parents or your grandparents were born. Then he tells us that every single one of us is made of the same stuff as stars. That's surprising, because *we* aren't burning balls of very hot, faraway light. But once stars burn themselves all out and can't shine anymore, they fling what's left of themselves out into the universe, and some of that stuff ended up creating Earth and everything that's in it.

I don't know how we will include all of this in our play. Maybe we will write about the distance between the stars and the Earth like the distance between a person writing a book and the person reading it—or like the distance between us and the undocumented girls. Our letters sometimes reach them after they have already left the detention center and we never know where they ended up, just like we don't know what happened to the stars that gave us their light. Sometimes I feel like the girls in detention are as far away as the stars, and sometimes I feel like they are very close to me. You can't see the starlight in Brooklyn, but when I read a letter from Dolores, it's as if I can feel her shining, even from very far away.

During the break, Talia takes out a bead kit. It has brightly colored string and enough beads for everyone. She had the idea that we could all make bracelets and then the next time our letters get delivered to the girls in detention, they could also get friendship bracelets from us. Most of us can't wait to get started on our bracelets, and the break flies by. Before we know it, Stephen is gathering us all around the table again and passing out more letters to everyone.

I cross my fingers and hope that there is a letter for me from Dolores. I imagine that she will tell me how she liked my unicorn and how she guessed that my father must be an artist because I drew her such a great unicorn. But after Stephen reads out all the names on the letters, there is no letter for me. Dolores hasn't written me a letter.

"The good news is that means she's not in detention anymore," Stephen tells me gently.

I know that's true, but I wish I could know for sure where she ended up. I miss the light of her letters. I wish someone could tell me that Dolores is with her parents. I wish someone could quiet the windmill in my mind.

There's one letter left, lying in the middle of the table by itself. Stephen slides it across the table to me, and I stare at the name on it for a long time. *Paloma.*

My friend Paloma used to come to Still Waters, but then she joined a soccer team and the practices are at the same time as Still Waters' rehearsals. Hopefully she'll come back sometime, but for now she isn't in our play. Whoever wrote a letter to Paloma won't get an answer.

Slowly, I unfold the letter to Paloma. It's from a girl named Alicia. She has drawn roses all over the paper. She is good at drawing.

We know that we won't always get an answer from the girls. We know that they are moving around, and anyway, we don't want them to be stuck in detention forever. When they don't reply, we aren't supposed to get mad—but I don't want Alicia to feel like I do now, with no letter in the pile for me. Even though Paloma can't write back, I want Alicia to get a letter with her name on it if she is still there when our replies arrive at the detention center.

I grab a new sheet of yellow paper from Stephen's pad, and I start writing. I ask Alicia if she has ever heard the idea that the library is a little bit like the universe—it has all the knowledge in the world. I tell her that you could think of each book a little bit like a person. Then I ask her what she thinks about libraries and universes. Maybe she has an idea that we could use in our show. After I finish writing I try to draw the best, most colorful unicorn I have ever made before. We learned today that the *uni* in "unicorn" is the same as the *uni* in "universe," and they both come from the word for "one"—like "*uno*" in Spanish. A *uni*corn has one horn and the *uni*verse is one place that unites us all together. So a unicorn is actually

a very good illus-
tration for a letter
about the universe.

After I finish
my letter to Alicia,
I help Cleo with
her letter. Her pen
pal is fifteen years
old and wrote
that she was feel-
ing sad and drew

an angel with a heart. Cleo writes back that she
would always stay with her inside her heart even
if they couldn't be together in person. She tells
her that in church she'll pray that she gets back
to her family. Then Cleo decorates everything on
the letter in pink—her pen pal likes pink, which is
Cleo's favorite color.

After we finish the letters and the bracelets,
Stephen organizes them and packs them up to
send to the girls. I look at the big manila envelope
filled with our notes and our drawings and the

beads we strung ourselves. The stars are far away from us, but we can see their light, and we are far away from these girls—but I hope they can see our light when they read our letters.

15

My Mother

When my mother was my age, she didn't live in a city, and she had already stopped going to school, because school was expensive and her family needed her to work. Her whole family spent day after day clearing grass and tending the *milpa*, which are the cornfields in Mexico. My mom worked outside even when it was very hot or she was very tired. She worked even when her muscles were worn out. She lived with eight brothers and sisters, her mom, and her dad. Some of my mom's brothers live here in Brooklyn, and

I see them all the time, but some of them live in Mexico, and I have never met them.

Because everyone had to work, my mom didn't get to go to middle school. Because her family was very poor, sometimes they only had tortillas with salt to eat, and they couldn't buy nice clothing. My mom admired the kids who didn't have to slog in the fields and went to school. They had beautiful uniforms that were always clean, and they had more energy, because they weren't worn out from farming and they had more food.

My mom told me a story about one time when she happened to be in the road, and some schoolkids walked by her. My mom was just minding her own business, appreciating their clothing and their book bags, when one of the kids started shouting insults at her. The schoolkids made fun of her because she didn't know how to read and write. My mom didn't cry, but she said she wanted to. She had only been thinking nice things about those schoolkids, and then they went and said mean things about her for no reason!

I think my mom was really a better student

than those kids, because even though she didn't have the opportunity to keep going to school, she kept trying to practice her reading and writing. Sometimes she would even take papers and pencils out of trash cans just so she could practice her writing when no one was looking. People didn't think that book learning was a very good use of her time, but my mom kept trying to learn. Unlike the mean kids she met in the road.

When I think about the stories my mom told me about when she was a kid, I wish I had a Time Stone, like Thanos in the movie *The Avengers*. If I had a Time Stone, I would go all the way back in time to when my mom was a little kid. I would make sure my mom didn't have to work hard and got to take plenty of breaks. I would make sure she had lots of water and clothing and anything else she needed.

When my mom was a teenager, someone called my grandparents and told them there was a job for my mom in Mexico City, otherwise called "el DF," which stands for the "Distrito Federal" or the Federal District, because it's the capital of

Mexico. Mexico City is a few hours away from where my mom lived in Puebla, and she went there all by herself. In Mexico City, my mom worked for a very wealthy woman. My mom took care of the lady's two children and helped her around the house. Even though the woman was very rich and had her own chauffeur and maid and nanny, she was a good person who treated my mom well. When my mom went home for the weekends, the woman asked my mom what her family needed in her town and sent my mom home with clothing for all of her eight brothers and sisters. When she realized that my mom wanted to learn to read and write better, she helped my mom practice. My mom was lucky to have a nice boss, and I think her boss was lucky to have her, because my mom is great at taking care of kids (I mean, she made *me*; she's got to be pretty good, right?).

Now that she lives in Brooklyn, my mom still has to work hard because she has to take care of my little sisters, and on Sunday she goes to work, but at least it's not outside in the hot sun. I get to go to school, and I have enough clothing. For my elementary school graduation, I'm even getting a brand-new dress that my mom is going to take me to pick out.

My mom makes all the special occasions more special. At Christmas she makes tamales, and last year she took Cleo and Natalia and me to see the tree at Rockefeller Center. Have you ever been there? It's an enormous Christmas tree, so big that you would think it was fake, but it's an actual real tree that happens to be as tall as a building. They decorate the tree with lights and an enormous star. It's across the river in Manhattan, so we took the subway to get there.

Sometimes I'm scared of the subway

because I saw a movie once where the subway cars crashed, but my mom tells me that's my imagination and I don't have to worry about the subway cars crashing. Bad things happen in the world, my mom says, "*Y a veces nos toca—pero a veces no.*"

What my mom means is that when bad things happen, sometimes we get stuck with the badness happening to us, and that stinks. But sometimes bad things don't happen, so she doesn't want me to worry about them, because they might not happen. If I'm always worried about them, then I might not get to enjoy the in-between times when the bad stuff isn't happening. *Cuando* no *nos toca.* It's easier said than done.

But, luckily, the subway ride went quickly. At Rockefeller Center it was so crowded with tourists that I was afraid of losing my mom's hand, but we all held on tight—Cleo, Natalia, my mom, and me. All the Sierra women except for Alma, who was a tiny baby and couldn't come with us. After we took a picture in front of the tree, we saw a light show projected on the building across the street from the tree. Somehow, there were patterns and designs of colored lights on the outside of the building, that jumped and danced and changed in rhythm to music that was playing throughout Rockefeller Center. Cleo said it made her think of a Disney fairy tale.

We had other adventures that day too, like going to the M&M's store in Times Square, also in Manhattan. It's like M&M's central. They had every color in the rainbow, and life-size M&M people that we took our picture with.

Even though I was born in New York City, I like going to places for tourists like Rockefeller Center and Times Square—especially with my mom.

16

The Morgan Library

I love field trips, and at Still Waters we get a lot of them. One Saturday, we get to go to the Morgan Library. It is the last in our big tour of libraries, and next week we will be hard at work writing our library scene. A lot of people in my family decide to come on this trip. Bernadette's mom comes and brings Bruno and Aldo, and my mom comes with Alma, Natalia, and Diego. A lot of other parents and siblings and volunteers come too.

We take—you guessed it—the subway, and I try to remember what my mom said about how *a*

171

veces nos toca y a veces no so that I don't worry so much about the subway cars crashing. When we get to the right stop in Manhattan, we walk the rest of the way to the library.

The Morgan Library is a two-story building made of gleaming white marble. It looks sort of small and out of place surrounded by the big sky-scrapers and office buildings in Manhattan. Kind of old-fashioned. A lady named Nadia meets us at the door. She is a museum educator, which means she's a type of teacher who works at a museum, because this library isn't a regular library where you can check the books out and take them home. It's a museum library full of rare, special books.

There are some rules we have to follow inside. All the normal ones, like no running or shoving or touching, but we also have to leave our bags and backpacks in cubbies because we're not allowed to have them during the tour.

First Nadia brings us upstairs in a glass eleva-tor. We wave down at everyone below us as the elevator rises through the air. Then we get to a sunny air-conditioned room full of windows.

Nadia explains to us that this part of the building used to be an outside courtyard, but then they covered it with glass so that people can use it when it's raining. It still feels kind of outside though—like, there are trees growing *inside* here. Percy points out that it probably makes the air better for everyone to breathe if there are trees.

Then Nadia leads us farther into the library. We enter a small room that is the exact opposite of the indoor courtyard we just came from. This room is dark, with a low ceiling and crimson-red wallpaper. The drapes on the windows look thick and heavy. There is a desk on one end of the room and a portrait of a stern man on the other. There are two red velvet couches, but a rope covers the cushions. You can't sit there. Nadia tells us that those couches have been there for a hundred years. No one sits on them so that they'll last another hundred years.

Instead, we all gather onto the carpet around Nadia. Even the grown-ups sit on the carpet. Nadia tells us about the man in the portrait. He was a banker named Mr. Morgan, and this library was his before he died and it became a museum. This room was his office, and he actually did his work at that desk. There wasn't a portrait of him though, they added that later. It would have been weird to have a portrait of himself. He could just look in a mirror instead.

Then Nadia takes us to another room that has books and glass cases full of interesting things. Some of the glass cases have little stone cylinders with carvings on them. We learn that thousands of years ago people used to use carvings to make clay stamps that they would wear around their necks. Mr. Morgan thought that was interesting, so he bought a lot of them from collectors. It must

have been fun for him, to just buy whatever interesting things he wanted.

Nadia tells us that, actually, Mr. Morgan
didn't always buy the books and the objects for
his library. Instead, he hired someone to buy the
things for him. He had an assistant named Belle
da Costa Greene. She traveled the world looking
for interesting objects and books for Mr. Morgan
to add to his collection. They didn't always agree
on what he should have, but usually, she made her
own decisions—sometimes Belle was on the other
side of the world and couldn't wait for a letter
from Mr. Morgan telling her whether to buy him
a book. She just had to trust her gut. Belle was a
black woman, and in 1905, she was just about the
only woman and the only black person working
as a collector of rare books and objects. She was
also the very best collector there was. When Mr.
Morgan was dying, he told her to find a way for
the people of New York City to enjoy his collection—and that's just what she did.

We pass a marble room full of carvings and

pictures on the walls, and Nadia brings us to the treasure room. This is the room we have been waiting to see all along. On one end of the room is a fireplace. The rest of the room is all books. There are so many books that there is a balcony with more books wrapping around the room on a second level. But there is no ladder! How do people get up there to see the books?

We all line up single file by one of the bookcases in the corner. One by one, Nadia tells us to close one eye and peek at the crack between the bookcase and wall. I see other kids gasp when it's their turn, and I wonder what could be so interesting. When I get there, I squint at the crack and *whoa*—there's an entire staircase back there, with lights and everything!

When everyone has had a chance to look we find out that the bookcase *moves*. Behind the bookcase is a secret staircase that the librarians can use to get to the balcony of books. Mr. Morgan didn't like using ladders to find his books, because he was old when the treasure room was built and he didn't want to go up and down a ladder. I guess he was worried he would fall. I think I might have put a ladder in my personal library—the kind that rolls along the shelves so I could glide across the room, way up high.

Now, it's time to see the treasures of the treasure room. Everyone is impressed by an enormous book in a glass case. The book's cover has sparkling jewels. There's another glass case with old books from Europe, illustrated with gorgeous colors. It turns out that back then, the colors for the books came from many different places, including precious gems. The blue color comes from a stone

called lapis lazuli, and the yellow comes from the most expensive spice in the world, saffron. The red color comes from a bug.

I'm serious! To make red dye, people used to crush up a beetle called the cochineal insect. Nadia shows us a picture of the insect and sure enough, it's very red. Then we find out that the cochineal insect lives by drinking the juice from something called a prickly pear.

That's what English people call a nopal, one of the volunteers whispers to us.

Wait a second! I know about nopal. It's a cactus that you can buy in Brooklyn and drink the juice inside. There are drawings of nopal leaves on a mural across the street from my apartment. Lotería cards have nopals on them. The nopal comes from Mexico!

I take a second look at those old European books in the glass case. Without the color red, the illustrations wouldn't have been very good. As usual, the Europeans are lucky they had Mexicans. Otherwise they wouldn't have nopals, which would mean no cochineal insects, no red dye, and

no beautiful illustrations (well, I guess their illustrations would have been okay, but the cochineal
insects from Mexico definitely made them better).

Finally, it's time for us to see the most important treasure of all. We follow Nadia to the one
glass case we haven't looked in yet. She points at
two thick leather-bound books. "Volume One and
Volume Two," she says. "The years 1605 and 1615."

I'm in the back of the group, so I stand on tip-
toe. I can't wait to see!

In his treasure room, Mr. Morgan had one of
the *very first copies* of *Don Quixote* to be printed.
You see, when *Don Quixote* was first published,
novels were basically a new thing. Really—before
that you could buy Bibles and plays, but novels
were pretty unusual. The printing press was new
too. So they didn't print a lot of books, because
that would have been hard, and they weren't sure
if people were going to like it. Think about it—
when *this* book that you are holding right now
is published, they will print thousands of copies. When *Don Quixote* was published, they only
printed like two hundred copies. And most of

those got lost or burned in a fire or tossed in the trash once the paper got too old. It was four hundred years ago, after all.

There are only, like, twenty copies left in the world of the first edition of *Don Quixote*, but Mr. Morgan's collector, Belle da Costa Greene, bought one of them for his treasure room. That book was published in 1605. But like I told you, Don Quixote is actually two books smooshed into one. Ten years after the first volume of *Don Quixote* was published, Miguel de Cervantes decided to publish a second book with more of Don Quixote's adventures. That's how it got to be such a long book—it's really two books in one. Mr. Morgan wanted the complete set, so he had Belle go out and buy him the second book too.

When it's my turn, I take a long look at the book. The words on the title page are very fancy. The paper is yellow brown, and even through the glass case I can tell that it is thick and heavy. Four hundred years ago, a man in Spain wrote this book, and now four hundred years later, in Brooklyn, I am translating and adapting his book.

After the tour, we all sit down to write in our notebooks. Stephen encourages us to write what we would put in our own personal libraries if we could build one like Mr. Morgan. Of course, I want marble ceilings and sculptures, and a trick bookcase with a secret staircase like Mr. Morgan had. And I would also have about five hundred different editions of *Don Quixote*—including the leather first edition from Mr. Morgan's treasure room.

17

I'm Going to
Middle School

Fourth grade is almost done, and next year I will be changing to middle school. I'll take the bus in the morning with Diego instead of with Cleo, and I'll change classes every period instead of just some of the time. Ms. Ajayi and Ms. Markovic won't be my teachers anymore. I'm excited to go to middle school. I'm not shy like I used to be, so I am confident about changing schools. I know now that I can tell the teachers if someone isn't nice

to me and raise my hand if I have questions. I'll
miss my really good friends at elementary school,
but some of the kids in my class right now are
different than they were when we were littler.
Now they get in trouble too much, so I'm ready to
make other friends. Besides, a lot of the kids from
my elementary school will be in my same middle
school anyway.

In April, we start state testing, and I realize we only have three months left of elementary
school! The first day of testing, everyone wears
the T-shirt with the design my dad and I made.
We are all nervous and worried about failing. But
the math test was *so* easy I think everyone in my
school did really well. Later on for the science test
we know not to be nervous anymore, because we
have already had the first round of tests. I like the
science test because during the lab section you get
to interact with all the different labs. There's one
with water, and I love the feeling of splashing and
feeling the water on my hands, even if it's for a
test. But either way, by the time we get through
all the subjects we are really bored, and everyone

just wants the testing to be over already.

I think even the teachers feel bad about how many tests we have to take, because as soon as the weather warms up, they start thinking of great things for us to do.

First we have a rematch of Math Olympics with the other fourth-grade classes. There are four classes in the fourth grade, and each one is named after a college. I am in the Saint Joseph's University class, and there is also Miami University, Hampton University, and City College. Earlier in the year we had a Math Olympics but we had to stop because of a fire drill, so after testing is over, we have a rematch. I cheer for the other kids in St. Joseph's when it's their turn to answer a question, especially for Gabby.

The next fun thing is that Ms. Ajayi organizes a slime party. We all get glue, conditioner, food coloring, and decorations like sparkles and tiny foam balls that make the slime crunchy. Then we start mixing. Some of the kids in my class were so bad during the slime party that the teachers had to send them to a silent table in the back of the room. Plus, their slime came out like a lump of hard clay because they didn't follow any of the mixing and measuring instructions. Luckily I have Makayla at my table, who is a slime expert. I'm serious; Makayla has made dozens of different types of slime and could mix the exact right proportions in her sleep. With her help, my slime comes out smelling and looking great. It is just the right amount of wet so that it's not crumbly but doesn't stick to everything either. We're allowed to play with our slime during breaks, just not during actual class time, so it's good to have our own slime stashes. Another day we have a spa day and make a hand rub that smells like lemons and flowers. It's too bad all school year can't be like it is after testing.

One day we have an all-school assembly for Ms. Facey, one of the deans of the school, who is moving so she can be principal at a school that's not doing so great and needs her help. Everyone cried during the assembly because we are going to miss her a lot. A lot of people shared favorite memories of Ms. Facey, like from before she became a dean, and when she was a music teacher and taught everyone to play instruments. Then the teachers and the second graders performed a skit about Ms. Facey and everyone cried more. It's almost like Ms. Facey is a fourth grader—we are moving to a new school next year, and so is she!

At the very end of the year my class is going to Hersheypark. We are going to get up very early in the morning and take a long bus ride to Hershey, Pennsylvania, which is where they invented the Hershey's chocolate bars. The people at Hersheypark are going to teach us how to make our own chocolate bars, and then we'll get to eat them, which is good because Ms. Ajayi and Ms. Markovic told everyone we can only bring healthy snacks on the bus. There's also a big amusement park full of rides. I don't like the rides that go upside down or go really superfast, but I do like rides that take you way up high. My favorite is a ride that looks like a giant swing set in the sky. You climb into a swing, and the ride lifts you up high. It swirls you around, but not too fast—it's like an airborne merry-go-round.

I love the feeling of being up above everything and feeling the air on my face.

To go on the field trip to Hersheypark, it cost a lot of money, and the money couldn't be a check— it had to be a money order, which is a type of check you have to get at the post office. My mom had to wait at the post office for a long time to get the money order for my trip to Hersheypark and my brother Diego's class trip to Washington, DC. It's funny, mine was more expensive than his, even though his trip is overnight. I was worried my mom would forget or that it would be too expensive because we both had trips, but last week my mom sent in the permission form and the money order, so I am officially going to Hersheypark. When I am in Diego's grade I bet I will get to go to Washington, DC, too. I don't know which I'm more excited about: summer break or end-of-the-year field trips.

18

Ten Cousins

How many cousins do you have? I have a lot. On my dad's side of the family I have so many cousins I can't count them, and most of them are older than me. But on my mom's side my cousins are all around our age and we are all friends (well, we have other cousins in Mexico, but we don't really know them except for pictures sometimes). I've already told you about my cousins Bernadette and Paulo. They come to Still Waters with Cleo and me. Bernadette and Paulo also have two little brothers, Aldo and Bruno, and we all have another little cousin named Lucas.

The ten of us are a very good team. Once, we were at a party in the park and we got separated from our parents—there were so many people, and one minute they were all right there and the next we couldn't see them. So all the cousins held hands in a big chain, then split up into two groups, with some big cousins and some little cousins in each group. We still held hands within the groups, and we walked around the park shouting until we found our parents and aunts and uncles. Then we were all reunited together.

It's hard sometimes being one of the oldest cousins, just like it's hard being an older sister. Sometimes I feel like I'm a traffic lady and a vending machine rolled into one because I always help the little kids cross the street, and I cut up oranges for them to have for a snack when they are hungry. Cleo complains that I should learn to make her favorite, lasagna, but I'm only ten. So she is stuck with orange slices until my mom or dad or one of our aunts makes lasagna.

I'm the oldest cousin on the school bus (Paulo, Bernadette, and Diego are all older than me, but they take a different bus to middle school), which means I am the official cousin captain on our school bus. At the beginning of the year my little cousins were acting wild, which was distracting for the driver, so Ms. Lovato, one of the deans, appointed me bus captain. Now I sit with Lucas, our youngest cousin, to keep him out of trouble, and keep an eye out for the other cousins while I'm at it. Cleo just sits wherever she wants with her friends, but I have a job to do, keeping an eye out for my cousins.

When I watch my cousins at home it can be extremely exhausting. Somehow whenever I think the little kids are busy doing something undangerous, they start roughhousing, and before you know it *I'm* in trouble for letting them! Sometimes I join in on the fun though, like when we have all-cousin pillow wars.

Once, there was thunder and lightning. At first we tried to keep the little kids from getting scared, but the lightning was so electric blue it looked like our whole apartment building would be sizzled up. The thunder rumbled so hard I worried the building would fall down. Then there was a *BOOM* that was so loud that I forgot what I was supposed to be doing and yelled:

"TAKE COVER!"

The little kids didn't need telling twice! They grabbed their blankets and pillows and dove under the bed and under the chairs. Then I had an idea—Diego and Bernadette and I helped turn the bedroom into a fort to protect everyone from the thunder and lightning. We used the pillows to pretend we were soldiers hiding in trenches, waiting out the enemy. I brought food and chips, and we stayed in our forts for a long time, until the storm ended. That day is one of my favorite memories. When all ten of us get together, we have a great time, even if we are stuck inside during a terrifying storm.

19

The Recording Studio

I will probably remember all the words to the songs in Kid Quixote forever. Cleo and I sing them all the time. When we're playing at home or walking from the bus, we sometimes sing the songs without even realizing. But the grown-ups seem to think that they might forget. They tell us they want to remember what our songs sounded like this year—the year Kid Quixote went on tour like a real theater company. So we're going to make an album of all the songs, and our families will be able to listen on their phones and computers forever.

This isn't a mom-recording-on-her-phone kind of album. This is a real album that we're going to make at an actual recording studio, like the kind where real musicians record. We're going on a field trip to get there. My dad is going to come with us this time, along with a few other parents, and Kim and Stephen, of course.

The day of the recording we gather in front of the gate at Still Waters. It rained the other day, and there are puddles around the edges of the sidewalk, where the water pools and can't get into the gutter. Santiago and Joseph get their shoes splattered while they kick around the soccer ball on the sidewalk. Percy is reading his book through his thick blue glasses. Bernadette and I bounce up and down to keep warm, chanting, "We're going to the studio! We're going to the studio!" When my dad shushes us, we all giggle.

We take the subway again, this time just a few stops to another neighborhood in Brooklyn. This neighborhood is busier than ours, with more shops and restaurants, but the street with the recording studio is quiet and narrow. There are old brick buildings on either side of the road. Lots of them have the metal gates down, which makes it feel like you are walking in the early morning, or at night. I know we are not in my neighborhood because none of the gates have graffiti as elaborate or as colorful as in our neighborhood. The studio is called the Bunker Studio, and my dad makes a joke that it's like a *real* bunker because the building is so hard to find from the outside. But once we get inside, the studio is actually warm and inviting. The walls and floors are made of golden-colored wood, and there are colorful carpets. Instruments line the hallway.

Inside the recording room we will be using, there is a table absolutely covered in buttons and controls.

"It looks like the cockpit of an airplane!" Cleo shouts, and rushes to sit down at the chair in front of the buttons. She pretends to steer. "Come on, passengers! Let's go!"

Everyone laughs, and some of the kids run

around. It takes a long time to get everyone to settle down so the man who works at the recording studio can give us instructions. He will sit at the chair in front of the control panel and wear headphones so he can hear how we will sound in the recording. We will all stand on the other side

of the room and sing the songs in our show one by one. We will record all the songs several times. Each time we record it is called a "take." Then, once we are done, the man will use all the controls to smoosh the different takes together—if we make a mistake on one line, it's okay, because chances are we are not going to make the same mistake on the *same* line on every different take.

Kim helps us warm up, and then listens carefully as we sing. Whoever has a solo gets to stand very close to a microphone, but everyone else in the chorus stands a little farther back. Cleo is having a silly day, because when she comes up to sing her solo she isn't quiet at all—she's loud—but instead of singing, "I followed the path of the singing coyote," she sings, "I *swallowed* the path of the singing coyote," and everyone bursts into laughter again. Here's the thing: that song is really sad, but when Cleo made that mistake, it stopped being sad and started sounding totally ridiculous. Maybe it's the same with my ICE people in underwear—when you make things funny they are less sad and intimidating.

It takes us a long time to calm down from laughing at the image of little Cleo *swallowing* a coyote, but eventually we get through six takes of all the songs, and Kim declares that we are done. The man asks us if we want to try on the headphones, and everyone rushes up to him for a turn. Kim and Stephen take pictures of a couple of kids wearing the headphones and singing into the microphones as if they are pop stars. It's going to take a long time to get the album we made back from the recording studio, because it's a lot of work to smoosh all those takes together.

On the way home, my dad and I talk about old movies, which is something we like to do. My dad points out that the Kid Quixote album might be around for a really long time, and even when

I'm an adult, I'll be able to listen to the music. It's like the movies my dad shows me at home. A lot of them were made when he was a kid, or even before he was born. But all my dad has to do is tap a screen a few times and he and I are watching the movie. It makes my head feel a little spinny to think about my voice being in something that will last such a long time. I scoot in closer to my dad, and Cleo scoots in closer to me. Whatever happens when I'm grown up, I like having my family's voices near me.

20

Mi Familia Is My Best of All

There are only two sessions left of Still Waters before we go on summer break. We spend them talking about the amazing library we are going to describe in the next part of our play. It will have rare first editions, books covered with rubies, secret staircases, and compact shelving. Our library will represent the universe, and the light from writers hundreds of years ago reaching us through their writing.

Cleo and I are the last kids to leave. I want to hang on to Still Waters as long as I can. I know I will be back in just a few weeks, but everything will be different then. I'll be in middle school!

Finally, we wave goodbye to Stephen, and I close the door behind us. As Cleo and I walk back to our apartment, we hear Stephen rolling down the gate. It will stay down the rest of the summer, keeping our place safe and still in the meantime. When it reopens, I will know my middle school teachers' names. I will perform the library section of our play. I might even see the silver roofs and rainbow houses in Mexico with my own eyes, because my dad is talking about taking me there to visit sometime.

I reach into my pocket as Cleo runs up the stairs to our apartment. My fingers wrap around something plastic. I pull it out of my pocket.

It's the flashlight that I use in the first scene of *The Traveling Serialized Adventures of Don Quixote.* I must have forgotten to give it back to Stephen after our last rehearsal. I use it when I pretend to stay up late reading at the beginning of the play. It's also the flashlight that Talia uses as the torch when she pretends to be the Statue of Liberty and we read the poem by Emma Lazarus that goes,

> *Give me your tired, your poor*
> *Your huddled masses yearning to breathe*
> *   free,*
> *The wretched refuse of your teeming*
> *   shore.*
> *Send these, the homeless, tempest-tost to*
> *   me,*
> *I lift my lamp beside the golden door!*

That's the poem that's on the base of the Statue of Liberty. It was written over a hundred years ago, at a time when there were many new

immigrants to the United States. They would arrive by boat, and as they steamed into the harbor of New York City, they would see Lady Liberty and those words on her base. In our play, we read that poem when I (as Kid Quixote) rescue the farm-worker from the cruel master. My friend Talia, who plays the farmworker, sings a song about how she came here seeking protection:

I came here to seek protection
I traveled through the night
Adios, preciosa patria
Found myself in burning light
burning, burning desert light.

When we wrote that song, all the kids at Still Waters pooled their knowledge of what it is like to come to the United States. One kid talked about their parents walking through the night, someone else shared their dad's story about what it was like saying goodbye to his *preciosa patria* ("beloved country"), and a few kids remembered their families telling them about how hot and dry it was in the desert, how the sun always beat down on them, all day long—*burning, burning desert light*.

Somehow, at Still Waters we are always talking about light—the space scientist who taught us about starlight, the burning desert light that immigrants walk through, the flashlight that lights up my book and is also Lady Liberty's torch. Sometimes light is welcoming, like when Lady Liberty lifts her lamp beside the golden door. Sometimes light is frightening, like when it scorches immigrants in the desert. Sometimes light helps us understand things, like when I read my book. And sometimes light tells you something about what's happening far away—like starlight tells us about other planets and letters tell me about what's happening to the undocumented girls. I like the last type of light best. I always want the light to be the kind that connects people, and makes them less far apart.

Lately, everyone is talking about the wall at the border between Mexico and the United States. The wall is supposed to split up families like mine—to separate my abuela from my mom and her grand-kids, to separate my dad from his father's grave, and to make us feel afraid. I shine my flashlight up the stairs of my apartment. I imagine that it's a light beam that can tear down anything it hits, and that it is hitting the border wall. As soon as the light touches the wall, it crumbles in half, and standing all around it is my family together. That is what light should do.

In the same scene where we recite Lady Lib-erty's poem and Talia sings her song, we also talk about the border wall. Talia sings,

Por favor, entiendan me!
Ignorance built this wall.
I don't want to live in fear
mi familia *is my best of all.*

When we wrote that stanza, we talked a lot about how ignorance, which is when people don't have knowledge, built the wall. People don't know about the families that are separated because of the wall, or about the jobs that don't get done because of the wall. They don't know, so they do terrible things—that's ignorance. It's what happens when people don't listen to other people. That's why our motto at Still Waters is "Everyone listens to everyone"—if you really pay attention to what other people say, you understand them. You show them that you respect them. If the people building the wall were really *listening* to kids, they would understand how cruel they were being.

The very last line of that stanza, after we say that ignorance built this wall, is "*Mi familia* is my best of all"—and I helped write that line. It was a long time ago, before Cleo started going to Still Waters. While we were writing that scene, the teenagers kept talking about different things that rhyme with "wall." I kept thinking about how sometimes the only thing that matters is keeping your family together. I thought about how nothing is worse than splitting up families, and that's what the wall does. I thought about my mom and dad and my brothers and sisters and my cousins and how I love them so much my heart wants to burst. So I scribbled down on my paper "My family is my best of all."

Of everything I like—field trips, tornado *crepas*, turquoise clothes, and old movies—there is nothing that is better than my family. They are my best of all.

Back then, I was still the kid who didn't say much. I was so little then, and all the teenagers were so big! But Lily, who is the teenager who goes to college now, was there then. She leaned over my paper and saw what I had written. Normally I wouldn't like people looking at what I had written, but Lily was different. She always helped me with my lines.

"Sarah has an idea!" she announced.

Everyone looked at us, and I read what I had written. It was so quiet you could hear a pin drop, because everyone was listening to everyone— including me! But even though everyone was listening, my voice still came out as a whisper. Now I know to speak out my lines, but back then I didn't. Luckily, Lily helped me read it aloud again so that everyone could hear it.

The teenagers all started talking at the same time. They liked the line I had written. They liked that it rhymed with "wall" and that it expressed the importance of family when immigrants cross the border. But it was still missing something. Families like ours don't just speak English. Most of us speak English and Spanish. But my line was all in English, which didn't sound right. It didn't sound like how we would say it at home.

Then Lily had the perfect idea. "Let's change *My family* to *Mi familia*," she said. "Then we have it all—English, Spanish, and family."

That's how I helped write the words "Mi familia *is my best of all.*"

I hum the words to myself and finally follow Cleo into our apartment. I put down the flashlight with the other things from Still Waters, like my big copy of *Don Quixote* and two letters from Dolores. I think about what I would say to Dolores if my letters could reach her now. Maybe I would tell her more about the Library of Babel, or about how starlight can reach us from so far away.

Or maybe I would tell her what we all sing at Still Waters after the farmworker sings, *"Mi familia is my best of all."* Our chorus responds with the words,

> *Can we help? Can we help? Can we help?*
> *We will protect you with our song.*
> *Can we help? Can we help? Can we help?*
> *We feel deep in our hearts you belong.*

I want to help all the families that don't get to be together because of distance or because of walls. I wish I were a real-life knight who could ride across the country with my horse rescuing people. Except I know that kids are a lot like Don Quixote, sometimes when we try to help we end up attacking windmills or making a lot of trouble. So for now, I live in Brooklyn with my parents, my siblings, my cousins, my aunts and uncles, my grandmother, and one survivor goldfish. After all, *mi familia* is my best of all.

I feel deep in my heart that Dolores belongs. I feel deep in my heart that I belong. And most of all, I feel deep in my heart that *mi familia* belongs.

Acknowledgments

First, I would like to thank my family, who always support me. I especially want to thank my mom and dad for everything they do. I'm glad my mom emigrated so I could have a good life here. I'm glad my dad is so supportive of my mom, like when she is looking for better work. Mostly, I'm glad for our family life in New York City. I also want to thank my cousins, because they know how much I want the program at Still Waters to keep going and inspire other kids—and for telling people about my book!

Thank you to Stephen Haff. If it hadn't been for his program, I would still be shy today, and I wouldn't have met so many amazing people. I love that because of the Still Waters program, I am Don Quixote and an actor. I also want to thank the other kids in the program for being so nice. Even with a lot of kids, there are no bullies. Thanks, everyone, for being friends and being so respectful of each other. Finally, thank you to the volunteers at Still Waters who support me and make me feel calm, and thank you for the art supplies, snacks, books, and board games.

I want to thank my elementary, middle, and future schools for giving me a great education and high standards so I can attend college someday.

A lot of people worked on this book! Thank you to Johanna and her assistant, Wendolyne Sabrozo. They made me so comfortable. Johanna speaks such fluent Spanish, which made my mom comfortable too. I never had to explain or translate anything, because Johanna was able to help. Thank you to the photographers, Michael Frost and Tom Schaefer; and to the book designer, David DeWitt, who made this book look great. Astrid Caballeros drew illustrations for this book that remind me of old times, family, and the program at Still Waters—I love them. Thank you to Emma Otheguy for putting me at ease with interviewing and book writing. To my friends at HarperCollins: thank you for publishing my book and making me feel like I am someone special whose story should be well-known by many people.